ALISTAIR COOKE ON...

BERTRAND RUSSELL

"He raged against the injustices of his fellow-men: of whom, from time to time, he greatly feared he might be one."

EDWARD VIII

"The most damning epitaph you can compose about Edward —as a Prince, as a King, as a man—is one that all comfortable people should cower from deserving: he was at his best only when the going was good."

ADLAI STEVENSON

"He remains the liveliest reminder for our time that there are admirable reasons for failing to be President."

H. L. MENCKEN

"It *is* true that he disliked puritans, teetotalers, Communists, Englishmen, Methodists, and politicians on principle. But if one presented himself who was otherwise a rational and agreeable man, he spontaneously filed and forgot his prejudice."

HUMPHREY BOGART

"Many first acquaintances were dropped at once when, out of shyness probably, they tried to adopt some of the Bogart bluster in the hope of showing right away that they were his sort. One of his sort was enough for him."

CHARLES CHAPLIN

"Neither in love nor in friendship did he ever tread water. He regularly took a header into deep water, and the splash usually shocked his envious neighbors."

ALISTAIR COOKE

WRITES ABOUT HIS FAMOUS FRIENDS

SIX MEN

BERKLEY BOOKS, NEW YORK

This Berkley book contains the complete
text of the original hardcover edition.
It has been completely reset in a type face
designed for easy reading, and was printed
from new film.

SIX MEN

A Berkley Book / published by arrangement with
Alfred A. Knopf, Inc.

PRINTING HISTORY
Alfred A. Knopf edition / October 1977
Berkley Medallion edition / November 1978
Berkley edition / November 1980

ISBN: 0-425-04689-3

A BERKLEY BOOK ® TM 757,375
Berkley Books are published by Berkley Publishing Corporation,
200 Madison Avenue, New York, New York 10016.
PRINTED IN THE UNITED STATES OF AMERICA

Photographic captions and credits appear on page 235.

The chapter on Edward VIII appeared originally in slightly
different form in *The New Yorker*.
The chapters on Mencken and Bogart appeared originally in
slightly different form in *The Atlantic Monthly*.

Grateful acknowledgment is made to the following for
permission to reprint previously published material:
Crown Publishers, Inc., and George G. Harrap & Company
Ltd: Brief excerpt from *The Later Ego* by James Agate,
edited by Jacques Barzun. Copyright 1951 by Crown
Publishers, Inc.
J. B. Lippincott Company and George Weidenfeld &
Nicolson Ltd: Brief excerpts from *Edward VIII* by
Frances Donaldson. Copyright © 1974, 1975 by
Frances Donaldson.
Little, Brown and Company in association with The
Atlantic Monthly Press and George Allen & Unwin Ltd:
Poem entitled "To Edith" reprinted from *The Autobiography
of Bertrand Russell, 1872-1914*. Copyright 1951, 1952,
1953, © 1956 by Bertrand Russell. Copyright © 1961 by
Allen & Unwin Ltd. Copyright © 1967 by
George Allen & Unwin Ltd.
The New York Times: Excerpt from an article by Harold Laski
reprinted from the December 7, 1936, issue of *The New York
Times*. Copyright 1936 by The New York Times Company.

FOR

Nunally Johnson

1897-1977

Contents

NOTE: In shorter form, the chapters on Mencken and Bogart originally appeared in the *Atlantic Monthly*, and the one on Edward VIII in *The New Yorker*. The chapters on Chaplin, Bertrand Russell, and Adlai Stevenson are quite new.

—A.C.

SIX MEN

A Note on Fame and Friendship

MORE THAN A CENTURY AGO, in his *Mirrors of Downing Street*, a collection of what were then called "character studies" of men in power, Harold Begbie put the quandary of the memoirist very succinctly: "Public men must expect public criticism, and no criticism is so good for them, and therefore for the State, as criticism of character; but their position is difficult, and they may justly complain when those to whom they have spoken in the candor of private conversation make use of such confidences for a public purpose."

In our day, the marketing of confidences "spoken in the candor of private conversation" has become a big and frequently disreputable business. An outraged victim can expect little balm from the courts, since the courts have decided that almost any act of license— from a scurrilous biography to filmed close-ups of

1

writhing genitalia—is just what the Founding Fathers had in mind to defend when they wrote the First Amendment to the Constitution.

Anyone who has been subjected to press interviews or, worse, to profiles "in depth" (usually composed on the basis of a two-hour conversation) knows that only very rarely does the printed piece approximate to a plausible account of the subject's views, let alone to a recognizable sketch of a character that is not a stereotype.

The intelligent complaint is not that the subject's vanity has been punctured, or—what as a general proposition is always true—that he dislikes being disliked. The flattering pieces are, in my experience, as unsatisfactory as the denigrating ones. Not from the interviewer's indulgence or ill will, but because a "profile" of anybody's character has to be so selective of obvious traits and passing impressions as to create not so much a false image as a synthetic original. It is, indeed, with such slick confections that politicians and movie and television stars have to come to terms.

I have tried to bear these things in mind. But Begbie is right. Famous men and women, by the act of putting themselves on display, whether as politicians, actors, writers, painters, musicians, restauranteurs, or whatever, invite public appraisal. They are all, impressively or pathetically, acting on the presumption that their ideas, their fantasies, their music, their bodies are more original than those of, say, a plumber or a certified public accountant. They are all exercising the impulse, as Mencken put it, "to flap their wings in public." This is so obvious to the critic—and, I believe, to the ordinary reader or spectator—that it seems hardly worth saying. But resentment of the practice of criticism itself is strong among professional artists (and all Presidents of the United States). There is a psychological type among them that hates critics *on principle* as parasites or failed performers. This is very natural but surely very childish and, in any country claiming to be civilized, actually antisocial. The existence of critics, good, bad, or indifferent, is a firm clause in the social contract between the governors and the governed in any nation that is not a dictatorship. Public figures should accept with good grace the public response to their invitation to be admired and resist the temptation to retort, except in the face of flagrant malice. The truth is that the constant reader, or viewer or listener, is usually prejudiced about the performer before the performance. If he likes you, he will like you all the more; if he dislikes you, he will dislike you all the more. Very few people who begin to read this book will, I imagine, have an open mind on more than one or two of its subjects.

Granted, then—I hope—that my own motives are, if not pure, at least circumspect, the reader will want to know *why* the choice of these six. I could say, truthfully, that they are six men I have admired and also liked. But the question that naturally follows is, how did it come about that I, who for much of the time was an obscure journalist, could come close to such gods as Chaplin and Mencken? The simple true answer is that of all the eminent people I have had occasion to run into, these six were the ones who most demonstrably took to me! I hasten to dampen the ardor of this egotism at once by saying that it is not difficult for political journalists in America, for foreign correspondents especially, to get on familiar terms with public men. Indeed, the higher the status of a politician, the more he seems to crave a good notice abroad. It is one of the hazards of our trade. Washington is haunted by the apologetic ghosts of once first-rate correspondents who became permanently disabled for the disinterested reporting of a President, or some other bigwig, after an early dose of intimacy. More than thirty years ago, I took a pledge with James Reston of *The New York Times*—my oldest friend in the business—to resist consorting with politicians beyond the bounds of acquaintanceship. Adlai Stevenson, I think, is my only case of backsliding. There were times when it was awkward to have to write freely about him, although I must say that when I took the risk, he was remarkably magnanimous, accepting a slap here and there as one of the prerogatives of my profession.

Stevenson, then, I should never have known if I had not been a foreign correspondent. Nor Bogart either, had it not been for the accident of a single assignment. As I later explain, I met Bertrand Russell at his own suggestion, a flattery likely to prejudice me in his favor from the start. But from that first meeting on, I had the same feeling as I'd had with Chaplin and Mencken: that I had known him most of my life and that we had been companions for countless years. As for Edward VIII, it would be absurd for me to pretend that I was ever more than a nodding acquaintance. I met him in private no more than three or four times, and got a citizen's glimpse of him in public on a score or more occasions. But he is a special case: a schoolboy's idol who left a lifelong impression (though mine on him, I am sure, left barely a trace), and a journalist's once-in-a-lifetime assignment to follow, at close quarters, the downfall of a King Emperor.

What is involved in such relationships is a form of emotional chemistry, so far unexplained by any school of psychiatry I am aware of, that conditions nothing so simple as a choice between the poles of attraction and repulsion. You can meet some people thirty, forty times down the years, and they remain amiable bystanders, like the shore lights of towns that a sailor passes at stated times but never calls at on the regular run. Conversely, all considerations of sex aside, you can meet some other people once or twice and they remain permanent influences on your life.

Everyone is aware of this discrepancy between the acquaintance seen as familiar wallpaper or instant friend. The chemical action it entails is less worth analyzing than enjoying. At any rate, these six pieces are about men with whom I felt an immediate sympat—to use a coining of Max Beerbohm's more satisfactory to me than the opaque vogue word "empathy."

In a professional life that offered many chances to meet famous men as far apart in time and character as Sigmund Freud and Jack Nicklaus, there have obviously been many other appealing subjects. I was tempted at one time to put together a gallery collection of living eminences whose characters and achievements are in the public eye. But if they are still active, they are always being written about, they are too close for a long view, and the present fashion in "people" journalism exposes them to immediate canonization or debunking. The business of revisionism—especially as applied to the big names since the 1940s—is now very lively. Churchill has been stripped of his halo and is being cut down to a size we can live with, when he is not being recomposed as one of the craftier causes of the Second World War. If I read the signs correctly, Kennedy's stature as a President is now about what it was in the view of people who suspected him from the start as the attractive but cagey son of a wily father. And I should guess that the deflation of Truman as a legendary, no-nonsense all-American is about due, and that his reputation will go down as Eisenhower's—long overdue for promotion—goes up.

These six men of mine are comfortably removed from the heat of idolatry or belittlement. The youngest of them—Stevenson—would now be seventy-seven, and the oldest—Russell—a hundred and five. Yet they all made a deep impression on this century, and their tracks are very visible in our time. André Malraux, in one of those blasting sentences with which Frenchmen love to seal off whole tunnels of inquiry, said that "the death of Europe is the central fact of our time." I don't know about that, but I am pretty sure that in their different ways these six sounded various tocsins: Mencken tolled the bell on the genteel tradition; Russell expected, single-handed, to cleanse the Establishment; Bogart was the first antihero hero; Stevenson, with noble naiveté, hoped to render obsolete the American political party machine; Chaplin did much to anachronize the tradition of the gentleman by parodying it on behalf of the dispossessed; and in the ordeal of Edward VIII we may hear the first death rattle of kingship.

So there are, I hope, objective reasons for finding much fascination in this sextet. Not to tie the reader down to a thesis, but to risk a suggestive generalization: they all seem to me to be deeply conservative men who, for various psychological reasons, yearned to be recognized rather as hellions or brave progressives. Perhaps that is their real link with this writer.

I

CHARLES
CHAPLIN

The One and Only

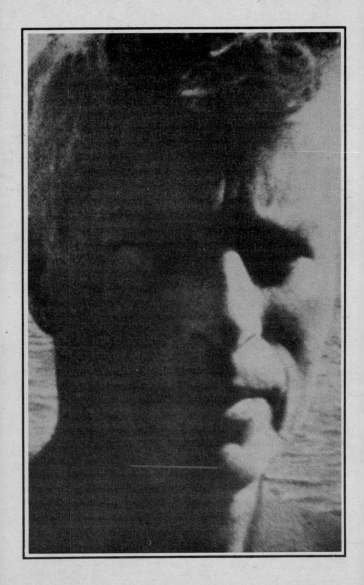

THE FANS. They sift around the entrance to the
Dorchester or huddle against a knifing wind on the
sidewalk outside the Broadway stage doors: miniature
traffic cops with their little books out, poised for the
kill. They palpitate up against the improvised stage on
any field large enough to enclose the pandemonium of
a rock festival. Like Olympic relay runners, they
stretch their arms to the limit over the barricades at
Wembley or Yankee Stadium waiting for the touch of
the afternoon hero. They used to mob department
stores where Sean Connery was rumored to be
shopping. I have seen them as a congregation of dolls,
bobbing behind the customs barrier at Tokyo, waiting
for the Rolling Stones to wing in from Seattle or
Hawaii. They are the distorting mirrors in which the
stars see their images blown up beyond any human
scale.

What this ceaseless adoration does to the psyche of the victims is something that the victims rarely seem to examine, though they reveal it in various touching or unlovely ways. They learn to practice self-deprecation by way of fake surprise. Or they bear with it as the inevitable codicil to a million-dollar contract. Or, more often than is pleasant to see, they wallow in the ocean of their narcissism and accept it as no more than the due of their uncanny beauty or talent.

But the fans today are not to be confused with the public. They are specialists, devotees of a particular cult that may be worldwide but is exclusive nonetheless. The disciples of Elton John have never heard of Giscard D'Estaing. Girls and matrons dizzy with desire for Robert Redford would not know Saul Bellow or Bjorn Borg, or maybe even Nelson Rockefeller, if they fell over him. Perhaps only Presidents of the United States and the Queen of England—Muhammad Ali dissenting—can bring out a general crowd, and then only during an election campaign or a coronation. Somewhere along the falling graph of our allegiance to authority, the general public seems to have exhausted its naive impulse to appear en masse for the arrival of the famous one—except in those "people's republics" where a million people can be commanded to appear on the double in the great square, or else.

But most of all, in our century, more people have come out everywhere to catch a glimpse of Charles Chaplin than did so for any other human in history. This sentence seems a contradiction: no celebrity could be seen by more people in more countries, though in the bacterial stew of the early cinemas, than Charlie Chaplin was. But he was the first world entertainer whose film persona seemed too real to be true: to see Charles Chaplin was to come face to face with the living Aladdin whose lamp had conjured up the genie we all loved and laughed at.

To say that anyone is the most famous, or the best, the greatest, the most beautiful, is—like all rhetoric—a method of bullying the reader into sharing a prejudice. The journalists who garnish a magazine profile with such superlatives, like the authors of screenplays about some chosen eminence (Pasteur, Beethoven, Sister Kenny), are writing from the focal center of their idol's local fame and assume that the din of it reverberates out from center to the farthest corners of the earth. This convention can produce scenes of hilarious innocence in the movies, where, say, an enterprising producer offers us a Parisian soirée at which our heroine George Sand is an invited guest. To foster a little desperate verisimilitude, the camera pans over the assembled company, and you get a glimpse of an Orson Welles bulk addressed as "M. Balzac," a passing remark addressed to a dandy with whiskers ("Tell me, Mr. Dickens"), a French lieutenant deferring to a fellow called Bismarck (no matter whether the Iron Chancellor had ever been in Paris or not). They are all hushed into reverence by the arrival of Merle Oberon in a tuxedo, for although the casual spectator may have thought of this as the Age of Revolution or the Reform Acts, he is meant to realize that the whole world swooned at the appearance anywhere of George Sand. In dull fact, George Sand and Charles Dickens, even with Bismarck in tow, could probably have roamed through Paris or London arm in arm and gone unrecognized by all but a chance acquaintance or an aficionado of daguerreotypes. Johnny Carson cannot go into a delicatessen anywhere between the Florida Keys and Fairbanks, Alaska, without a chorus of oohing and ahing and a rush of autograph hounds.

A year or two ago a New York magazine concocted

a list of the 100 "most famous men and women in the world." By the most generous count, not more than a dozen of them could have been heard of outside the regular readers of the American editions of *Time* and *Vogue*, the nighttime audience for American television talk shows, dentists' patients, and the addicts of *The New York Times*'s proliferating gossip columns. The composers of the list had plainly ignored the fact that our world includes the inhabitants of Europe, Communist China, and Upper Volta, not to mention all of South America and Australasia.

Yet Will Rogers was saying nothing but the literal truth when he wrote, in 1931, that "the Zulus know Chaplin better than Arkansas knows Garbo." Throughout the 1920s and into the early 1930s, Chaplin was the most famous man on earth. It is impossible to pick another person of any nationality to whom such a legion of other international celebrities was eager to be introduced. At one time or another, they included the Crown Prince of Japan, Woodrow Wilson, Prince George of Greece, Nijinsky, Lord Louis Mountbatten, Franklin Roosevelt, Georges Carpentier, Diego Rivera, Albert Einstein, Pandit Nehru, Pablo Casals, Nikita Khrushchev, Jean Cocteau, and Chou En-lai.

As early as 1917, when Chaplin had been making two-reelers for only three years, his studio was the court to which trooped the most eminent of touring artists: Paderewski, Godowsky, Heifetz, Harry Lauder, Dame Nellie Melba. In 1921, on his first return to Britain since he had left it as an obscure vaudevillian, the crowds at Waterloo lifted him on their shoulders from the boat train, and the streets along the three-mile route to the Ritz were lined as for a coronation. Ten years later, over 100 police were required to guard him between the Tokyo docks and the Imperial Hotel. On a two-month visit to Europe in

1931, which included a short detour into Africa, he had
to abandon shopping expeditions in Algiers and
Marrakech. In Berlin, he was the guest of the
Reichstag. In Paris, the Briand Cabinet attended his
investiture into the Legion of Honor. In London, he
was toasted at a public banquet by Winston Churchill,
and among the great ones who sought him out were H.
G. Wells, J.M. Barrie, Emil Ludwig, Lloyd George,
Lady Astor, the King and Queen, the Prince of Wales,
the Duke of Connaught, and Bernard Shaw. Shaw
broke a lifetime's vow by wearing evening dress to
appear with him at the opening of *City Lights*.
Mahatma Gandhi was the only innocent in this
majestic procession of fans. Told that it was important
for him to meet the great man, he replied, "Who is Mr.
Chaplin?" He saw him nevertheless.

This celebrity list is not compiled to elicit gasps of
astonishment. It is meant merely to sharpen the point
that whereas the Beatles, for example, may have
enjoyed an idolatry as widespread, it was only among
their fanatical followers. Chaplin was mobbed by
ordinary people of all types, of all ages, was known to
every country, and was the sought-after guest of kings,
statesmen, authors, artists, celebrities of every sort.

It has to be borne in mind as a burden on the ego
quite beyond the imagining of the rest of us. There is
one story that Chaplin loved to tell which shows that in
the beginning no one was more overwhelmed by the
extent of his fame than Chaplin himself. This may at
first sound suspicious as fact and coy as a confessional,
because we think of fame as something that burgeons
and can hardly amaze its object, unless it mushrooms
overnight, as with Lindbergh.

It happened to Chaplin when he was already
earning $1250 a week, a salary which would have been
handsome enough for an opera star. (Within a year, he

13

signed for $10,000 a week.) He was, at the time, the most financially precious property in the movies. But it is hard for us now to appreciate how inbred was the American motion-picture business in its infancy, how much of a colony in exile its practitioners had created.

In 1915, there were studios on Long Island, in Chicago, and in the hills across the bay from San Francisco. But Hollywood, only four years away from the status of a sheeptown without a post office, was already the world's motion-picture factory. It was all so new and so self-absorbed in its productiveness that its workers formed as parochial a community as the scientists laboring in their hideout in Los Alamos to make the atom bomb. An Englishman I knew for many years who had gone out to Utah in 1908 to look over his father's investment in a copper mine, and who subsequently drifted to San Francisco and tapped a little silver in the Tonopah strike, used to exercise his horse by signing up as an extra for the primitive Westerns being made at Niles Canyon by "Bronco Billy" Anderson, a partner in the S & A (for Spoor and Anderson) company, which, as Essanay, signed Chaplin to a contract that quadrupled his former salary. This worldly Englishman told me how he had struck up a friendship with Mabel Normand, an early and beguiling film comedienne, and how he went down one time to Santa Monica to watch the shooting of a Chaplin film in which she appeared. For two or three days—which was as long as it took in those days to do the whole filming—he hung around with the cast and dined with them in the evenings. He must have been as flattered as any other European visitor to be socializing with the legendary "Charlie." But he told me what a shock it was to notice the crudity of Chaplin's table manners, his brusqueness with waiters, his cocky assumption that he was the smartest moviemaker in town. Which indeed he was, even though his conceit was a kind of bluster covering up the rueful knowledge that he was no more than a big fish in a tiny and socially rather murky pond of Southern California.

On lonely evenings—and Chaplin always prized the good artist's retreat into the loneliness that breeds ideas—he liked to go over to a favorite café in Santa Monica owned and run by one Nat Goodwin, a light comedian who had long ago established himself in London as what Max Beerbohm, among others, thought of as the supreme "American mime." Goodwin had retired to California and there looked back with anecdotal amusement over the ease of his theatrical fame and the strain of eight marriages, one of them to Maxine Elliott, a mountainous beauty whom he recalled as "the Roman Senator." Chaplin knew all about Goodwin's fame and looked on him, no doubt, as the first among equals. He went to Nat Goodwin's café as to a court and listened to the King recall his triumphs. But Goodwin was far more aware of Chaplin's fame than Chaplin was.

There came a time in the beginning of 1916 when Chaplin was exhausted by the frantic routine of making thirteen films in fourteen months. He had just finished cutting *Carmen*, his parody of the opera, and he decided to accept the invitation of his brother, Syd, to rest and play in New York. It would be the first time he had seen the big city since he had left it as a member of Fred Karno's vaudeville company. Goodwin told Chaplin that he would be lionized and gave him a little avuncular advice: "You'll be invited everywhere, but don't accept. Pick out one or two friends and be satisfied to imagine the rest. . . . John Drew was a great favorite with society and went to all their houses, but they would not go to his theater. They had had him in their drawing rooms."

15

Well primed by this cautionary tale, Chaplin boarded the train for the journey east and relaxed into the five days of anonymity that would precede the social whirl he had been warned to expect from the actors and actresses and social-theatrical hangers-on in New York. On the evening of the second day, he was standing in his underwear, shaving in the washroom, as the train pulled into Amarillo, Texas. He was aware of a vague baying sound as the train slid into the station. He peered out and saw a dense crowd on the platform and a line of trestle tables piled with refreshments. Like any other traveler, he assumed that Amarillo was out to welcome some local hero—a football star, the Governor perhaps—and he went back to his lathering. The baying sound came into focus as a chant: "Charlie! Charlie! Charlie! Where's Charlie Chaplin?" There was a rush of footsteps along the corridor and a deputation caught him. He was allowed to wipe his face and pull on a shirt and tie and descend to a roar of cheers, as the Mayor stepped up to invite him to "have a drink and a light refreshment" with, apparently, the entire population of Amarillo. At any rate, the crowd was too boisterous for safety, and the Mayor, slammed against the train with a rumpled Chaplin, as the cops strode and shouted, performed a Groucho switch of mood and snapped, "All right, Charlie, let's get it over with."

In the retelling of it, Chaplin recalled this line as the one delightful memory of what had been a trauma. When it was all over, and the train moved off, he sat in his compartment, huddled against the pointings and gigglings of the people who had lately seen a fellow passenger and now recognized a marvel. He was, he would admit, at first wildly flattered, then frightened, and, long before New York, facing for the first time the fact of universal fame and the psychological problem, peculiar I imagine to ventriloquists, of being worshiped as the creator of a being outside himself.

It was the same in Kansas City and Chicago. Along the route, where the train ran through suburban stations, people stood in clusters or long lines beside the track waving at the Man who must be in there somewhere. It was no longer the Southern Pacific transcontinental daily out of Glendale. It was the Chaplin Train, as one would say the Lincoln Train.

From then on, he had to learn to acquire the protective affability, and the stoicism, that recognizable celebrities must live with. It was not easy for him. He discovered with some alarm that he cherished his privacy, which was now invaded night and day. He was also highly opinionated, and while he responded extravagantly to anyone who sincerely sought advice about some private turmoil or the future of capitalism, he was insulted by general questions that might be put to any other celebrity, and he was rattled to the point of outrage by gossip-column queries about his taste in women, in food, whether he would ever play Hamlet or become an American citizen. He refused to perform for a shipboard concert. At Cherbourg, a ship's reporter wondered whether he considered Lenin or Lloyd George the greater man. He snapped, "One works and the other plays," thus planting an ominous hint of other innumerable offhand sallies that would get him into a thicket of public squabbles in the years ahead.

When he had acquired some self-possession, which he once admitted to me deserted him most often when most he needed it—namely, in the presence of newspapermen out to bait him—he was most concerned to dispose briskly of the interview, the war bond speech, the balcony appearance, and lock himself into his privacy. This impatience to have done with the adulation—which he once significantly remarked "is

given, after all, to the little fellow, not me"—brought
him unfairly the reputation of a misanthrope. Simply,
but hopelessly, he discovered, after the first return to
New York, that he could enjoy no such luxury of
choice as Nat Goodwin had recommended: "Pick out
one or two friends and be satisfied to imagine the rest."

For, it is fair to say, the next twenty years or so, the
shoals of mail (in London 73,000 letters in two days)
never ceased, nor the flood of invitations, nor even the
celebrity-seeking raids of other celebrities. It forced his
private life to be surreptitious, and few public figures
had for so long such a continuously turbulent private
life. From his earliest slapstick days, when director,
cast, actors, and crew were vagabonds, there was
always some mischief brewing with one or other of the
Mack Sennett bathing beauties. Chaplin, it should be
remembered, was not only a dapper and amusing man,
an enchanting mimic from childhood on. He was also
remarkably handsome, extremely attractive to women
and instantly susceptible to them. To two types more
than most: the *femme fatale* and the child-woman. The
gamut is represented at its polar opposites by Pola
Negri (for all that she was born Appolonia Chalupek)
and his first wife, Mildred Harris. Time and again he
found himself involved with earthy, lusty women. But
the ones he sought were nubile adolescents. He
married three of them: Mildred Harris at sixteen, when
he was twenty-nine; Lita Grey at seventeen, when he
was thirty-five; Oona O'Neill at eighteen, when he was
fifty-five. I state this as an interesting but probably
inexplicable emotional pattern.

MOST OF THIS, all the accumulated detail of his fame as
the one and only Charlie Chaplin, was known to me—
and much of it was flooding through my mind—on a

still and brilliant midsummer morning in 1933 when I sat on the deck of a yacht anchored twenty-odd miles southwest of Los Angeles Harbor, looking across the shimmering water to the small mountainous island called Catalina. The yacht was, by Riviera or even Hollywood standards, modest, a fifty-footer Chaplin had named the *Panacea*. There were five of us aboard. Chaplin, then forty-four. Paulette Goddard, an enchanting twenty-two-year-old brunette, as trim and shiny as a trout, whom Chaplin had known for little more than a year. Andy, the skipper, a gnarled, good-natured man of few words (and a former Keystone Kop). And Freddy, a Japanese cook. And there was I, a lean, black-haired twenty-four-year-old Englishman on a two-year fellowship at Yale. In another place, or applying for a job on paper, I would have explained that I was a young man of mixed but lively aspirations to be either a theatrical director of the stature of Reinhardt, Piscator, or Meyerhold *or* a playwright of deafening fame (I was undecided just then whether to be the acknowledged successor to Noel Coward or Eugene O'Neill). But sitting there for the first time on anybody's yacht, waiting for my host to wake up and emerge from the bacon odors misting up from the galley, I was a fortunate nobody immersed in a glow of vanity, wondering, as the reader must be, how I had got there.

This is a thought which brings up, as dazzling accidents do in everyone's life, a sequence of unanswerable "ifs." If, on my arrival in New Haven, Connecticut, toward the end of 1932 I had not written out of the blue to J. L. Garvin, the venerable editor of the London *Observer*, hinting that I was well qualified to write occasional reviews of the New York theater; if he had not agreed; and if, when I brashly proposed a six-part series of articles on Hollywood, to appear in the summer, his celebrated film critic, Miss C. A. Lejeune, had not arranged to take a six-week holiday, thus providing a hiatus which I could neatly bridge, I should never have met the great man. But I no sooner had Garvin's consent than I sketched out the series under five heads (director, cameraman, shooting on location, English star, and Chaplin—just Chaplin), and wrote off letters of request to Ernst Lubitsch, Lee Garmes, George Cukor, C. Aubrey Smith, and Chaplin. (The choice of Smith as the English star may now sound odd, but I was writing for an English paper, and at that time he was symbolizing the British Empire to a gaping world a good deal more heroically than Stanley Baldwin. I got a charming handwritten note from him, provoked perhaps by my having mentioned that my father remembered him warmly as "Round-the-Corner-Smith," a sporting tag he had acquired, long before his acting days, as a famous amateur England cricketer. He was a bowler with a peculiar run-up to the wicket that has not, so far as I know, been imitated since: starting at eight o'clock, he ran down and around a fishhook curve up to one o'clock and then delivered the ball. Since, from the batsman's point of view, he started way right of the umpire and then suddenly appeared close to his left side, Smith offered the menacing illusion of being two bowlers instead of one.)

The last reply to come in was a curiously cordial letter from one Alfred Reeves, manager, telling me that Mr. Chaplin would be pleased to see me if I would appear at the studio office at ten o'clock on a certain morning in July.

Chaplin's reputation was the Caesar of independent producers, a multimillionaire, and a ferocious disciplinarian hatched in my fancy a vision of his studio as easily the most imposing of the Hollywood lots, patrolled between pictures by a private army of guards and subservient underlings. I was frankly nervous when I drove along Sunset Boulevard in my $60 secondhand Ford and watched for the turnoff into North La Brea. I drove past the studio several times before checking with a nearby lunch counter, whose owner assured me that the address I had scribbled down was indeed that of the one and only Chaplin studio.

It was a row of linked brick-and-stucco cottages, one with a turret, another with a Victorian bow window, two chimney stacks, four gables with imitation beams of brown-painted wood. My dented Model A seemed exactly right. Righter still was the little man who greeted me, Alfred Reeves, a wiry, courteous Cockney sparrow, impossible to place in any fantasy of the Hollywood hierarchy as anything but a gaffer, a carpenter maybe, one of those strange, self-contained Englishmen one meets in the unlikeliest places in America, who must have been fired at some point by the rumor of the American dream and who settle for a lifetime in a humble job without any apparent sense of disillusion.

Alfred Reeves had come over on the ship with Chaplin and the London vaudeville troupe, and until he died he was Chaplin's only manager. He offered in person a first proof of something very appealing about his boss. Chaplin could sustain outrageous feuds with business partners, drop old friends on a whim and walk in on them again with a grin, issue imperial edicts banning this titan or that from his studio, and summarily jilt houris both obscure and famous. But he was unflaggingly loyal to his old-time staff, in the manner of a sergeant who has been through years of trench warfare with a motley pack of privates and ever afterward uses them as a protective base of sanity

21

against the fits and starts of the higher-ups. At least a half dozen of the vaudevillians who appeared in the earliest Chaplin primitives could be spotted in character parts a quarter century later. As the most creditable example, there was Rollie Totheroh, who was Chaplin's cameraman at Essanay in 1915. As Chaplin became Shaw's "one artist of the cinema" and moved out of two-reelers into the grandeur of full-length feature films, with a correspondingly grander investment to protect, it would have been entirely sensible for him to cast around for new and spectacular talents. But Totheroh, a diffident and thoroughly competent craftsman, was still there shooting *Monsieur Verdoux* thirty-two years later. He was there, in fact, on the day of my arrival, filing some old prints and pottering around in a leisurely fashion, on full pay, though there would be no more filming for another two years.

Reeves took me off into Chaplin's office, another shock but one softened by the inoculation of the first: the row of workers' mock-Tudor cottages which constituted the facade of the studio itself. The office was the central room of a small bungalow. It had worn oilcloth on the floor, and if it was ever wallpapered, the paper had rotted in the fungi of mildew. There was one small window, three straight-back wooden chairs, an old table, about half a dozen books with peeling spines, and an ancient upright piano hideously out of tune. It was probably about as luxurious as any of the rooms Chaplin rented in the boardinghouses of prewar England, and as I was to learn, in working there the following year, it reflected Chaplin's deep distrust of elegant surroundings whenever there was serious work on hand. It was also, it now strikes me, the reassuring home base that some men whose childhoods have been grindingly poor require in the years of their affluence.

Chaplin himself had noticed the same trait in Bronco Billy Anderson and may have caught from him the courage to indulge it ("It was dark when we entered his bungalow... the place was empty and drab. In his room was an old iron bed with a light bulb hanging over the head of it. A rickety old table and one chair were the other furnishings. Near the bed was a wooden box upon which was a brass ashtray filled with cigarette butts.... This was the home of G. M. Anderson, the multi-millionaire cowboy").

Reeves was saying something about Chaplin's frequent burnings at the hands of the press but how, for some unstated reason, "this is different and he'll be happy to see you," when the man himself stepped smartly through the door and came into the room. The first impression was of being suddenly with two optimistic midgets in the office of a failing vaudeville agent. Neither Reeves nor Chaplin could have been much over five feet. We exchanged the usual nervous grins and "Well, well!" handshakes, and Reeves, assuring himself that Chaplin was in an affable mood (the precaution of a swimming teacher who is satisfied that the children are playing safely at the shallow end), bowed out and left us alone.

You expect a small man to have a small hand, but it was not until you doubted for a moment whether it was flesh you were holding or some ivory knickknack that you looked up at its chuckling owner and said to yourself, He certainly is a tiny man. His feet were in scale, peeking out like mice from under high-held trousers. Above the trousers were a white angora sweater, and above that a tanned face, small ears set flat behind the cheekbones, gray eyes of a dancing mobility, and above them a monumental forehead and hair piled like a melting snowball. I like to think I would have been arrested anywhere by the face:

features evenly sculptured into a sensuous whole, strong and handsome beyond any guess you might have made by mentally stripping away the black half-moon eyebrows and the comic mustache. This startling disparity between Chaplin and "Charlie" might be thought to have protected his identity from the fans, and I remember once, coming out of a movie theater with him, how a young man nudged his girl and hissed, "There's Charlie Chaplin!" She made the obvious comment that it didn't look like him, to which the young man irritably snapped, "You can't expect anybody to *look* like Charlie Chaplin." In the early days, he could wander incognito through the cities of California. But by the time of that first railroad journey east, the news of his presence anywhere was so trumpeted in the papers or by word of mouth that people had to see him in order to believe that the creator of the immortal tramp was the same person in another guise. So seeing Chaplin for the first time was a more curious pleasure than having the screen image of any other star confirmed in the flesh.

Reeves's notion that this press interview would somehow be "different" was explained by the sort of lucky coincidence that can transform a wary first meeting into a starting friendship. Reeves had warned me that Chaplin, after a spate of more or less scurrilous articles about him (the papers had made a messy thing out of his second divorce), had cut himself off from all access to the press, thereby compounding his normal isolation from Hollywood and all its denizens. In the two summers I spent with him, the only movie people—the only people, for that matter—who ever appeared at the house were King Vidor, Frank Reicher, an old German character actor, and Dr. Cecil Reynolds, his stagestruck doctor.

On his recent visit to England, Chaplin had been

warmly entertained by the Astors, who owned the paper I was writing for. He had also struck up a congenial relationship with another Alistair, the son of Prime Minister Ramsay MacDonald. It was as simple as that. At any rate, the "interview" dissolved into lively conversation, and from there we went to lunch and then up to his house, where I was introduced to "my friend, Miss Goddard." A routine mannerly hint from me that I ought to be on my way was brushed aside, and through the long afternoon we sat round the empty swimming pool (there was a polio epidemic that summer), and I left at sundown on a promise to be back next day to dinner. After that, I was up at the house almost every day, and then he invited me for a weekend aboard the *Panacea*.

It was the beginning of a friendship that was as close as could be through that summer and the next. But I come back to the first cruise on the *Panacea*, because during its four or five days Chaplin opened himself up in the most natural and revealing way, and very little that happened afterward was much of a surprise to me. The impression I picked up then, confirmed later by other close friends—Frank Reicher, John Steinbeck, and more than any other Dr. Reynolds—was that when Chaplin took to anyone, he was wide open from the start, spontaneous, generous, gabby, confidential, as if taking up again where he had left off with a favorite, long-lost brother. I could see then how, if it were a woman who attracted him, he would soon be as deep in intimacy as Macbeth was in blood and find "returning as tedious as go o'er." This instinct to plunge into a relationship with all the defenses down can be darkly ascribed to a helpless reflex of egocentricity. And Chaplin undoubtedly needed to dazzle a new friend with the whole panoply of his charm, humor, talent, knowingness, and—which was a little less impressive to anyone used to thinking—his intellect. But, instant psychoanalysis apart, it ought to be said that whatever the spring of its motive, it was a warming thing to receive. There was nothing of the poltroon about Chaplin. Neither in love nor in friendship did he ever tread water. He regularly took a header into deep water, and the splash usually shocked his envious neighbors. Much of the public uproar about his matrimonial troubles came from highly moral women's groups, who, no doubt correctly, felt their own marriages threatened by the possible contagion of Chaplin's gallantry. In his auto-biography, and looking back from the cool sanctuary of old age, he put it very succinctly: "Procreation is nature's principal occupation, and every man, whether he be young or old, when meeting any woman, measures the potentiality of sex between them. Thus it has always been with me."

Looking across to the little boats bobbing gently by the quayside at Avalon, I was startled by a deferential cough and turned to see Chaplin standing over me. He had come up from below as lightly as a grasshopper and was standing there in the attitude of a butler awaiting orders, head cocked expectantly, a napkin over the left forearm, his right hand poised in a kindly-step-this-way freeze. It was the silent movie call to breakfast, and we went below. I have seen only one other man dispatch a meal with such speed. But whereas Adlai Stevenson, belying his general reputa-tion for delicacy, shoveled the stuff in with hands as pudgy as baseball mitts, Chaplin disposed of eggs and bacon and a wad of pancakes almost as a display of sleight of hand. One of the permanent pleasures of being with him was to watch the grace and deftness with which he performed all physical movements, from pouring syrup to swerving like a matador just out of the line of an oncoming truck.

"My friend, Miss Goddard" was not yet up, so we took the dinghy and rowed over to the shore and went for a walk. I suppose we were gone for no more than a couple of hours, but in them he managed to elaborate on most of his life, as if he were doing the first rough dictation of a biography or giving a deposition by free association. "I am the renowned Charlie Chaplin," he seemed to say, "and you are a new friend who might well turn into my Boswell. Very well, let me begin to tell you some things you ought to know."

He told it in no sort of sequence but began touching base with me on his recent memories of England, and from there went into flashbacks of his childhood and youth. He started by making it plain that in spite of his hobnobbing with royalty, with the Tory leaders in London, and international socialites on the Riviera, he was neither a royalist nor a Tory and, what's more, took the standard radical view that in forming a national government, Ramsay MacDonald had betrayed the Labor Party and was not much more than a lackey of what today we call the Establishment. All this was a little puzzling to me, for I was at the time about as apolitical as it is possible to be, and I have been amazed, in going back through the political history of Britain during the years I was at Cambridge, to see how casually unaware I was of budget deficits, the American debt problem, the departure from the gold standard, and other weighty matters which Chaplin went hotly on about as he sat squeezing the sand between his toes in the hills above Avalon.

This was not quite what I expected of the world's ranking clown, and he must have guessed that my ahs and ums and other grunting responses proceeded from no very deep conviction or even from a passing acquaintance with the facts and dogmas he trotted out. But I often noticed at other times that he was anxious to tell strangers what he was *not taken in by* rather than to say where he stood politically. (All his life his much-abused "radical philosophy" was no more than an automatic theme song in favor of peace, humanity, "the little man," and other desirable abstractions—as humdrum politicians come out for mother love and lower taxes.)

But I had been in Germany two summers before and seen all around me the blue faces and bloated bellies of starving people. I had enough political instinct, however uninstructed, to sense the depths of despair from which the mass of people could look up to Hitler as to the only possible savior. And I had just driven halfway round America and told him how roused I had been by the contrast of a listless nation suddenly galvanized into energy and confidence by Franklin Roosevelt. Roosevelt! I had made the connection: the dense pupil suddenly says a bright thing. He was all for Roosevelt, believed he had saved the country from revolution, and saw the New Deal as a promising halfway house on the road to "true Socialism," which, I gathered, was not Ramsay MacDonald's spurious brand but something on which Joseph Stalin had the only legitimate patent. (In his autobiography, Chaplin is frank enough to leave in the recollection of a conversation with H. G. Wells, whose fears of dictatorship and the suppression of civil liberties in Russia are dismissed by Chaplin as growing pains or tactical "mistakes" not to be compared in grossness with "the repudiation of foreign loans.") There is an interesting psychological point here. Chaplin always talked about capitalism as a more or less failing system and showed no anxiety about its doom. But I was told by people who knew him as a businessman that he was as alert as a radar specialist to the rise and fall of the stock market. He told me, that summer, in a moment of offhand pride, that he had felt in his bones the coming of the 1929 crash and astutely transferred his holdings to Canada and South Africa and other places where the collapse was less painful. He had, he once boasted, lost little or nothing in the Depression.

I was beginning to think that actors, like writers and opera stars, were never the same at home. Certainly, the world's funniest man would have turned into the world's most hectoring bore if he had gone on and on even as long as these recollections. But I have, unfairly, lumped his political sermons into a running credo. He was always reciting them in snatches, at the unlikeliest times, and in the end they led to his banishment from the United States, an outcome that no one could possibly have predicted on that August morning as Chaplin preached to the Catalina hills and to me. But a funny memory of the First World War incidentally revealed on that occasion a wound long forgotten in England and, I should guess, hardly known about in the United States. As soon as Chaplin had established his no-nonsense political credentials, he fell into reminiscences of the old music-hall songs, and, cued by my mention of some of the great gone names, he went off into a bout of marvelous total recall, ballooning before my eyes into the bosomy swagger of Marie Lloyd and bawling out "A Little of What You Fancy Does Y'Good," then shrinking into the exquisite shape of Vesta Tilley, the pocket Astaire, and singing "I'm Colonel Coldfeet of the Coldstream Guards" and "Into a cookshop he goes dashin',/Who should bring his plate of hash in,/But the girl he had been mashin',/By the sad sea waves." I told him that my father had kept for me, and I still had, a wartime record of "Oh, the Moon Shines Bright on Charlie Chaplin."

"That," he said, in sudden alarm, "scared the hell out of me."

What I'd forgotten in mentioning that song, though it was neither hard nor pleasant to recall, was the insensate jingoism of wartime Britain, the hounding of German shopkeepers, the cretinous women patriots handing a white feather to young men in civilian clothes, and the holy indignation of comfortable editorial writers against any famous Englishman abroad who had not dashed home to join Our Boys Out There on Flanders Fields. Chaplin was a glaring target, and there was much doltish sarcasm at his expense, until it was discovered that few imports from England bucked up Our Boys Out There like the Chaplin films shown behind the lines. For a nasty spell he was Chaplin the Slacker in the London press and "Good Old Charlie" in the trenches, after which the hunt was abandoned. At its height, somebody sent Chaplin the new song. In its American original it was about an Indian maiden called "Little Red Wing," but the lyrics were changed in the British version, whose chorus went:

Oh, the moon shines bright on Charlie Chaplin,
His boots are crackin'
For want of blackin',
And his little baggy trousers they need mendin'
Before we send him
To the Dardanelles.

"I went home," said Chaplin, "and read about the Dardanelles after that, and for a time I was certain they were out to get me." He laughed now, but he had remembered it as a threat long enough to begin hustling around addressing war bond rallies with bouncing enthusiasm once the United States was in the war.

The songs led naturally to the old vaudeville days in England and the seedy rooms, in dark provincial towns, that he had shared with Stan Laurel. I don't think he saw much of Laurel in Hollywood, certainly not in my time, but he spoke affectionately of him and told me why. There was a time during a provincial tour when Chaplin was often absent from his lodging, till one Saturday night he came back petrified with fright that his girl in the show was pregnant. Laurel evidently confronted this life crisis as mildly as he contemplated the crasser ordeals of Oliver Hardy. He went off to his trunk and fumbled round in it for a while and came back with a handful of pound notes. They were such savings as he could have scratched up from a fifteen-shilling-a-week salary. Chaplin never said whether the offer had to be taken up, but the memory of it made him more indulgent to the antics of Laurel and Hardy than to any other of the Hollywood comedians, of whom he was uniformly contemptuous. The Marx Brothers were just then getting into their swing, and Chaplin was almost defensively scornful of them. "Nothing but anarchists," he'd say, which—considering the implicit anarchy of his own film character—suggested that Chaplin thought the best way to mock society was not to fight it but to join it by way of parody.

He talked in a touching and rambling way about his childhood, but neither then nor ever later did he moon over his poverty or sentimentalize the groveling times (he left the tearful touch, regrettably, for the heroines in his movies). As he went on, acting out with great spirit and delicacy his early attempts at shabby

31

gentility when he got into vaudeville, and then went further back to miming a wealth of characters fixed forever in his boyhood—in the workhouse, the pickle factory, chemist's shops—I had the odd feeling that I had heard and seen all this before. Charles Chaplin was Charles Dickens reborn. As documentary support for a thesis merely, there is the eerie similarity between *Oliver Twist* and the first sixty pages or so of Chaplin's *Autobiography*. But as a reincarnation of everything spry and inquisitive and Cockney-shrewd and invincibly alive and cunning, Chaplin was the young Dickens in the flesh. I had started to read Dickens when I was not more than nine, and by the time I was twelve I had gone through all the novels and whatever I could lay my hands on by way of memoirs and biographies, from Forster and Dolby to Mamie Dickens' *My Father as I Recall Him*. I was so absorbed in his fictional world that the streets I lived in were more alive with Dickens characters than the actual humans who peopled them. If I ever mentioned this to Chaplin, I can't now recall it. He would have been only mildly interested. I doubt he ever read any fiction; he was too busy manufacturing it.

For the rest of that cruise he was in manic good spirits. We fished for swordfish with mackerel, and catching nothing, and being fresh out of mackerel, we then fished for mackerel. I had just bought an 8 millimeter movie camera, and with his extended thumbs touching and his palms at the parallel he would fix the frame for me and retreat to mime a range of characters he picked up from the headlines of the only newspaper we had brought aboard. Jean Harlow had just eloped, and I still have Chaplin's outrageous cameo of the happy, if bewildered, bride. A famous female impersonator had been given a "friendly push" and drowned, a disaster which, however harrowing in

life, was reenacted by Chaplin as a neat and ribald
playlet. The Prince of Wales was seen to be making a speech: Chaplin tugged at nonexistent cuffs,
acknowledged the thunder of the mob, licked a
nervous lip, and bobbed his head in nervous modesty
from side to side: almost a prevision of the melancholy
future King.

Chaplin had a mild but steady obsession with
royalty, some secret need to deflate it in mimicry, as if
he would thereby expose the hypocrisy of hereditary
thrones as compared with the one he had constructed
with so much sweat and talent. He had dined with the
royal family, and one time he was going on about the
anachronism of monarchies in the twentieth century.
As always, the sermon was prolix and dull, but the
dramatization of it in mime was wonderful. He
remembered having once seen a newsreel of Edward
VII coming out of the house at Sandringham before a
shooting party. Chaplin walked ahead of the invisible
retainers, froze his stance, and very slowly raised his
elbows in a position to receive his cape. He never
looked behind him but gazed confidently out to the
horizon, slumped his shoulders as the cape descended,
gave a heavy grunt, and—for all Chaplin's tiny
gymnastic form—was the huge patrician buffalo to the
life. After that, there was no need for moralizing tags
about the arrogance of empire, the absolute assumption of hereditary superiority to the human clay that
cooks the meals, beats the bushes, mines the coal.

Chaplin was so relaxed on that cruise, so naturally
restless and inventive, that in retrospect I can see he
was revealing himself as if by describing an endless
series of Rorschachs. One thing led on impulse to
another, and after some talk about the future King
George VI and his stammer, Chaplin suddenly asked
me to take some photographs, both still and in motion,

33

of himself as Napoleon. (The frontispiece to this chapter is one of them.) He pulled his hair down into a ropy forelock, slipped one hand into his breast pocket, and slumped into a wistful emperor. He started to talk to himself, tossing in names strange to me—Bertrand, Montholon—and then took umbrage, flung an accusing finger at me, and, having transformed his dreamy eyes into icicles, delivered a tirade against the British treatment of him on "the little island." His face was now a hewn rock of defiance. I have it still on film, and it is still a chilling thing to see.

It will occur to the reader, and it has been said time and again with tedious clairvoyance by people who disliked him, that the trouble with Chaplin was a Napoleon complex. We are on touchy ground here. Tall men make a habit of explaining a lively sex life in small men as a crippling Napoleonic fantasy, though in my experience the small men seem to hop from bed to bed with singular and enjoyable agility. The truth in this instance was that Chaplin had been thinking for some time of doing a film about Napoleon on St. Helena. And he was serious enough about it to write to me the following winter and say that if I was free to come out to Hollywood the next summer, he would like me to do the research and help him with the script. Needless to say, I jumped at it, and drove out from Cambridge, Massachusetts, to Hollywood, set myself up in a room at the Mark Twain Hotel, and again presented myself, this time as an important employee, to Alfred Reeves. Now it was possible to get close to another Chaplin, to the professional, to one as far removed in action from the social Chaplin as a jolly general from the same man preparing the invasion of France.

He came scurrying into the bungalow every morning on the dot of ten in cap, tieless shirt, white slacks, and the angora sweater; sat down at the creaky little table; and said, "Shall we go?" For a week or two, I fed him stuff from books I'd picked up at the public library, with Las Cases' *Memorial of Saint Helena* as the principal source book. Then we started the script, and the first thing he taught me was that you don't begin at the beginning. "We look," he said, laying down the law with a firm index finger tapping the table, "for some little incident, some vignette that fixes the other characters. The audience must never be in any doubt about them. We have to fix them on sight. Nobody cares about *their* troubles. They stay the same. You know them every time they appear. This is no different from the characters who surround 'the little fellow.' *He's* the one we develop." (This, by the way, sounds like another Dickens prescription.)

Sometimes we had along Carter De Haven, whom Chaplin had hired to be assistant director on *Modern Times*, which was then beginning to brew in Chaplin's mind. Almost always, except during the knottier historical stretches, there was his massive old friend, spiritual uncle and adviser Henry Bergman, who had played in some of the early two-reelers as every sort of foil from a fat lady and a bum to a pawnshop owner. Bergman was a huge, gentle old German to whom Chaplin always referred some promising scene or gag. He said very little, but if Chaplin had doubts, in the moment of improvising, he would look over to Bergman, say, "No?" and Bergman would shake his head, and we'd forget it.

In the ramshackle bungalow, whenever we were stuck, Chaplin would pace around, mimic all the parts, mutter variations on a line I'd written, inflect it this way and that, sigh, smoke, stroke the piano keyboard, and say, "Let's try again after lunch." We went off always to the same place, Musso Frank's, and Chaplin made a point of banning all talk of the script. At the end of the meal, he would make a silent sign to Bergman, who produced the money and paid the bill. I never remember Chaplin carrying money, and once I asked him about this. He put it down to the childhood days when he was being shuttled between the workhouse and various board schools, and to the memory of his father, who, if ever he appeared with money, would exhibit it as proof of solvency at last but would then blow it in a drunken evening. Chaplin told me how when he was first offered $60 a week to go to Hollywood, he thought the money was a bribe and would never last. Years later, when he barely knew he was world-famous, he lived in a room at the Hollywood Athletic Club, until one day his brother, Syd, took matters into his own hands. "Look," he said, "it's crazy for you to go walking down the road always looking for a cab, you're a rich man. Buy yourself a car." They finally went downtown to a showroom, where the first thing Chaplin saw was a large, high sedan. Chaplin, telling this, went at once into his act of the high-hat millionaire commanding empires. "Tell me, my good man, is that a good car? I want nothing but the best." It *is*, said the man, *the* best. Chaplin waved an imperious wrist: "I'll take it." But it took his brother another year to get him to move out of the Athletic Club into a house, which he had steadily refused to do. "Syd, I remember, put on his coat and had one last try. He begged me to go and consult my bank balance." They went off together, and Chaplin was appalled to discover he had upwards of $900,000 in a checking account. "You see," roared Sydney. "You can *buy* yourself a *home!*" Chaplin went out and bought himself the one and only home he ever lived in in Beverly Hills. "But," he said, riding back to the studio in a Rolls, "I don't trust it, I still feel it'll never last," and chuckled.

Script sessions are as nerve-racking a bit of committee work as any board of directors ever has to face. One bad day, when I was being more than usually obtuse about how some tricky scene could be resolved into sight as well as sound, Chaplin gently suggested, like a doctor to a dithering hypochondriac, another, possibly more soothing, form of treatment. We would go for a stroll through the relics of the sets for *City Lights*. We gazed down into the arid cement basin which had been his suicide's intended grave. We walked along the embankment. He sat down on the stony bosom of the unveiled statue, which was now lying on a broken plaster elbow. And he started to go over well-remembered scripting crises in *City Lights*. A famous one will suffice to show what agonies of sweat and tension could go into the distillation of a scene which in the playing seemed as effortless as quicksilver.

"I began," he said, "with a hazy idea of a blind flower girl sitting on the sidewalk. She is going to be the heroine. And this is the first time the little fellow meets her. She must sell him a flower, and she must mistake him for a rich man. That's what I started with." He gave this simple rundown to his assistant, who drafted some sequences that conveyed the general idea. They were filmed, argued about, and destroyed. Chaplin sat down in the bungalow and tried again and again. "I was a terror to be with," he said, and I could believe it. He paced around the bungalow, flew into quick rages, refused food and rest, dragged his assistant by night to the house, and tried again. He shuffled every conceivable formula employing girl, flowers, sidewalk, rich man, poor man, five-dollar bill, expensive automobile, police whistles, crowds. He shot these fumbling scenes and found them as clumsy as the others. "Then, one day I wondered how the girl—a blind girl—could possibly be aware of the automobile." It took three weeks for the sparking detail to occur that would animate the whole idea. "I came down one morning, very glum, a bear, and I looked at the automobile and it hit me: *a slamming door!*"

All that happened in the end was that the tramp approached the girl, and as he did so, an automobile braked against the sidewalk. Its occupant walked rapidly to the park railings beside the girl. The tramp bought a flower and tendered his last dollar bill. While he was waiting for his change, and she was feeling for it, the smart steps retreated to the car, she heard the door slam and the purr of a luxurious engine. She hesitated, said, "Thank you, sir," and the tramp, distraught about his vanished change but not wanting to shatter this pretty vision, backed away on tiptoe. In the finished movie, the incident flowed like water over pebbles, smooth and simple for all to see with no hint of the groaning pressure that had gone into it.

But these agonies exacted a high price from his friends, his staff, and all his business relationships on the outside. When any such script crisis was unresolved, he would retreat to the house, alone or with one assistant, and give his Japanese servants the sternest orders that he was home to nobody and would not answer the phone. He would call up the faithful Alf Reeves to say he was out to anybody who might call, write, or cable. Reeves would then make a list of every outstanding social or business commitment and send the word out, to cronies and board meetings alike: "He can't see you and he won't talk to you. And if it's any consolation, I'm on the blacklist, too."

When Chaplin started to brood over the script of

The Great Dictator, the Los Angeles police department was using all its regulation ingenuities to get in touch with him. They had a little matter of a subpoena to discuss. One Michael Kustoff was claiming that Chaplin had plagiarized the story of *Modern Times*. The process servers started by knocking on the front door and subsequently tried getting in as laundrymen, doctors, and Western Union messengers. Months later, the courts finally gave up and the judge signed an order to allow the subpoena to be served by publication.

If anything, the moment of release from filmmaking was worse, for Chaplin's friends, than the throes of creation. He felt that the easing of the strain relieved him also of the social obligations he had ignored or postponed. One afternoon, after a tense but rewarding session with the Napoleon script, he asked me back to the house to relax "and mooch around the piano." We got to arguing about Shakespeare. Chaplin never overcame the prejudice that Shakespeare is an unactable poet and that on the stage his language is as embarrassing as the theatrical conventions of opera. The previous winter, I had directed a theater group at Harvard in *Cymbeline* and done it in modern dress as a scandal in the diplomatic corps in Rome. By this device, it had come to life again as a rich and malicious Noel Coward comedy. It satisfied me anyway, although it shocked the critic of the Boston *Evening Transcript* into a fatal coronary. Chaplin was fascinated by this idea, called for some tea, and asked me to read the play aloud to him. I read on into the twilight, by which time I knew he was supposed to be on his way to a party that Sam Goldwyn was throwing in his honor. I looked at the clock and reminded him. He erupted into a fury and stalked around the room like the outraged Little Corporal himself: "A party!

Good God, what is a cocktail party, and a bunch of Hollywood ninnies, compared to this? You'd think they owned me! The one thing that money gives you is the right to change your mind and do what you want, *when* you want to do it. Keep going!" (It was a trait I noticed later in other very poor boys who had grown very rich: a willful desire to flout the idea that there is any such thing as a duty or a social obligation.)

About an act later, he bared his teeth and gave the slit-eyed grin that made him look like a jolly Oriental. "I think," he said, "I'd better call poor old Sam." The moment he was connected, he startled me by begging to be excused in a voice croaking with advanced laryngitis. It was a pathetic sound. He was deeply sorry, in more misery than he could tell, he'd been hoping against hope the thing would clear up, he would surely call the first day he felt he was going to survive. He hung up the phone, made a large mock-heroic gesture, and cried in a resounding baritone: "On with Iachimo, let's get to the adultery!" We read on until midnight, when he thought it would be amusing to have supper at a geisha house he knew in Los Angeles' Little Tokyo. The proprietor's voice at the other end was fawning with delight. So Chaplin routed out his chauffeur, Kono, from a deep sleep, and we were out until three in the morning. (Eight years later, I ran into Kono sitting at the door of a wooden shack with a handkerchief over his mouth against the swirling dust storms of the Owens Valley. He was one of the Japanese-Americans who had been carted off to the concentration camp, discreetly called a "relocation center," in Manzanar, on the eastern, the safe, side of the Tehachapi Mountains.)

By THE END OF THE SUMMER, we were coming along well
with the Napoleon script, and one evening I was up at
the house playing piano duets with him of *Titine*, which
he was to use in *Modern Times*. After a break, he came
back into the living room, took out a toothpick, sucked
his teeth, and said, "By the way, the Napoleon thing.
It's a beautiful idea—for somebody else." He said no
more, and we never wrote another word or referred to
the project again. It was the same with two other ideas
he had during the summer. One was to be "a film
revue," containing three or four short films. He got
very excited, for several nights, with the notion of a
nightclub scene in which the floor show was to be a
dead-solemn miming of the Crucifixion. Another was
the old French legend of "Our Lady and the Tumbler,"
the slight and tragic sketch of a starving tumbler taken
in by a nunnery. In gratitude for his care, he goes into
the chapel but is ashamed to offer up his ignorant
prayers, so he gives his all, by way of his tumbling
talent, and breaks his back. As he lies dying, the Virgin
comes down and blesses him.

Chaplin simplified the whole legend in his head and
one night mimed it for me—the stumbling prayers, the
shamed interval, the half-comic realization that his
acrobatics could be enough of a tribute: for positively
one evening only, he was every shape and name of
humility. But he didn't bring it up again, and when,
days later, I dared to, he said almost snappishly, "They
don't pay their shillings and quarters to see Charles
Chaplin doing artistic experiments. They come to see
him."

AT THE END OF AUGUST, 1934, I was to be married. My
father-in-law to be was the President of the American
Public Health Association, which was holding its

41

annual meeting in Pasadena, and so that was the obvious place for the ceremony. I asked Chaplin if he would be my best man. His alacrity in consenting was touching, and he made much comic play, as the day approached, with the imagined disasters of a marriage service that misfired.

When we got to the Pasadena registry office, my father-in-law was already there talking to the magistrate. Quite simply, Chaplin never showed up. Luckily, a Harvard friend of mine, who lived in Pasadena, was along, and after an hour's fretful wait, he stood in for me.

Days went by before I dared to call the house. Kono told me that "Mr. Chaplin has gone with Miss Goddard to Arrowhead." There was no other word. But the following evening, I called again and Chaplin came on as blithe as a robin. When was he going to see the bridal couple? Where and when should we hold the wedding party? We must come up to the house at once.

Without ever referring to his nonappearance at the marriage ceremony, he walked up and down in bubbling spirits, setting the date we'd dine and dance at the Coconut Grove, and nothing would do but white tie and tails. So it was, and we had a marvelous evening, with Chaplin the soul of friendship, courtesy, tenderness, and drollery. This was apparently the first time in many months, if ever, that he had taken Paulette to a nightclub, and she came alive and shining at the prospect of breaking with some regularity out of the Chaplin cloister-on-the-hill into the high life. If that was what was on her mind, she was soon dismally disillusioned.

The midnight show at the Coconut Grove was coming to its end in the usual melancholy atmosphere of reeking smoke, flat champagne, and lovers staring at the table and having second thoughts. The star performer was one Gene Austin, a sugary crooner who had an alarming, but highly admired, habit of modulating his final notes a whole octave higher and so giving out the sound of a boy soprano or castrato. "Revolting," muttered Chaplin, who had declined into a brooding silence. Riding home, Paulette kept up the heartbreaking pretense that from now on her evenings would be agog with music and dancing. Chaplin gave her a black parental look. He started in about the cacophony of jazz, which he hated, and went on about the decadence of night life, the excruciating "eunuch" sounds to which we had been subjected, and the fate, similar to that of Sodom, which would shortly overtake the Republic. Paulette saw her vision collapse like the Ghost of Christmas Present. A tear ran down her enchanting face and her eyes fairly popped in frustration as she said, "What are we going to do evenings—stay home and *write theses?!*" Well, Chaplin replied, "One night a year is enough of that rubbish."

At the house, his spirits revived, but there was no champagne to help them along. He never, through the two years I knew him best, drank or offered any alcohol. To make things worse, he enforced this abstinence on his guests not from forgetfulness but from evangelism. He ordered his man to fetch a huge pitcher of water and the required number of tumblers. Our wedding party ended on a scene that would have warmed the heart of a Southern Baptist. We sat there yawning slightly, throwing in monosyllabic responses to Chaplin's elegy on the modern world, and took long meditative drafts of pure cold water. It did not help to recall an old and feverish Sunday school song: "My drink is water bright, water bright, water bright!"

However, before we left to go east, and from there on to England and my first job—as the BBC's film critic—Chaplin came down alone to our hotel, took dinner with us in our small suite, and was his gentle, brimming self. At one point, he motioned me out onto the terrace overlooking the hills and asked me quite directly if I would like to stay and be his assistant director on *Modern Times*. Though shocked into a daze of vanity, I replied just as directly that the Commonwealth Fund, whose fellowship I had been holding for the past two years, required that all fellows return to some part of the British Empire for at least two years. (I later discovered that the fund would have waived this requirement at the mere mention of a job with Chaplin.) He thought it was a pity, and then said an astounding thing. Apparently, it was not a training in film direction that he had in mind. "If you stay with me," he said, "I'll make you the best light comedian since Seymour Hicks." Hicks was then as adroit a light comedian as any on the English stage. But a comedian still. As I have mentioned, I was thinking just then of becoming Eugene O'Neill. We thanked the maestro warmly for all his kindness, and I went to bed still marveling that an artist of Chaplin's sensitivity and lightning perceptions could offer to cast O'Neill as a light comedian.

AFTER THOSE TWO MEMORABLE YEARS, I saw him only intermittently, the last time in a London restaurant, where I was dining with his publisher and mine. He was off at a table with his wife and several children, but he came over and sat down, and though he was now in his late seventies, he shed the years as he reminisced and chuckled, and—as I recalled the first passage on the *Panacea*—he threw his head back and crooned with a faked bronchitis: "Oh, the moon shines bright on

Charlie Chaplin...." He was the old incomparable charmer again.

I saw him not at all during the bad years of the late forties and early fifties, and this is a memoir, not a life. But I ought to say something about them, if only for people too young to have picked up much more than the rumor of Chaplin's pesky "radicalism." I told earlier how the implied threat of the old song about the Dardanelles had genuinely scared him, and how—whether reacting to that threat or not—he had been a busy seller of war bonds once the United States was in the First War. In the Second War, he sold no bonds. And he conspicuously turned down all invitations to perform at USO concerts and the like. Closeted in Beverly Hills, he became a fairly unpopular figure in the movie colony, especially among the male stars who had not joined up and were all the more anxious to prove their machismo and their patriotism by "morale" tours of army camps. In 1942, Chaplin came out of his isolation and, in a single act of misjudgment, laid up years of grief for himself.

He yielded to an invitation to replace the ailing former American Ambassador to the Soviet Union and address a rally in San Francisco for Russian War Relief. After that, heady with the pride of having turned in one night from mere funny fellow into political spellbinder, he made a long-distance telephone speech to a Madison Square Garden mass meeting that was sponsored by the Congress of Industrial Organizations. It had the support of such simon-pure Americans as Wendell Willkie, the 1940 Republican presidential candidate, and Mayor Fiorello La Guardia, who was an early speaker. It was admittedly a rally to urge the opening by the United States and Britain of "a second front" to relieve the

Russian armies sagging on the eastern front. With these two speeches, which blazed with unqualified praise for the gallant Russians ("On the battlefields of Russia democracy will live or die!"), Chaplin probably sealed his dubious reputation among old America Firsters and other professional patriots who were, within a decade, to rise again and bedevil prominent liberals, as well as crypto-Communists, who could be shown to have been "premature" (i.e., pre-Pearl Harbor) "antifascists." At any rate, when the country recoiled, for good reason, from the old American-Soviet alliance in the early years of the Cold War, Chaplin's number was up, both as an off-the-cuff public speaker and as an adored public entertainer. His first postwar film, *Monsieur Verdoux*, was at first banned by the Motion Picture Association's censor. In its final form it was picketed vigorously by Legionnaires, had a rocky short run in New York, and provoked a spate of abuse of Chaplin as a renegade, a "fellow traveler," if not actually a secret Communist, and a "paying guest" of the United States who, in spite of paying out millions of dollars in American taxes, was an ungrateful alien who ought to be thrown out of the country.

He was harassed and investigated for several years. Nothing could ever be dredged up to show that he was other than the "nonconformist of no political party" he had always claimed to be. No indictments were ever handed down. After releasing *Limelight*, he packed for a holiday in Europe, and he and his wife boarded the *Queen Elizabeth* on the seventeenth of September, 1952. Once the ship was well out at sea, the United States Attorney General rescinded Chaplin's reentry permit on the vaguely rhetorical ground that he was "an unsavory character" about whom the Department of Justice had "plenty of information available." If so, it was never authenticated or even made public. Chaplin was left in the now familiar limbo of rumor and untested assertion, until he had had enough and chose his own exile by turning in his reentry permit to the American vice-consul in Geneva. I had it from the Solicitor General of the United States two years later that Chaplin's politics had nothing to do with the excluding order, and that there were no constitutional grounds on which he could have been deported. Some people, unidentified, in the government "felt" that he had come close to deportation in a paternity suit he had lost. Others "felt," on no evidence I could adduce, that he had been chronically cavalier with such things as subpoenas and so had shown contempt for the courts and laws of the United States.

In short, he was a vague nuisance, and a tiresome talking point among the noisy patriots who never felt that the government's "loyalty" procedures proceeded far enough. Chaplin was all the more offensive in that he could never, after endless investigating, be pinned down as a criminal. He was simply turned in—by, we should remember, the Truman administration—as a useful sacrifice to the witches who were then supposed to be riding high exclusively on the broomstick of Senator Joseph McCarthy. The Chaplin expulsion was a squalid episode in a shabby period. The most accurate and honorable account of it I ever read appeared in—of all improbable places—a Madrid daily during the heyday of the fascist Franco.

The film industry, which in the scary decade after the Second War had hastened to keep him at a distance, the better to take a dim view of him, made it up to him in a stagy, sycophantic way when he was in his eighty-sixth year and had practically to be carried across the ocean back to the country he had loved and come to deplore. They gave him a special Oscar and a dinner in his "honor" in New York. As the crowds surged around him in Lincoln Center, and the televised Hollywoodites rose and pounded their hands, he shuffled carefully to a microphone and forlornly wished them well and said in not much more than an amplified whisper that he loved them all. The tears drenched the audiences 3000 miles apart. He was very old and trembly and groping through the thickening fog of memory for a few simple sentences. A senile, harmless doll, he was now—as the song says—"easy to love," absolutely safe to adore.

II

EDWARD VIII

The Golden Boy

ON A WARM AND SUNNY midsummer morning in 1932, the Prince of Wales had as the first official engagement on his calendar a reception for the latest batch of Commonwealth Fellows.

The Commonwealth Fund was a foundation set up by an American philanthropist, Edward S. Harkness, with the intention of spending the great fortune his father had acquired as a partner of John D. Rockefeller. In the beginning, the money went mostly to medical research, to hospitals and libraries in Latin America and elsewhere, but in 1925 the fund created its fellowships, to be awarded annually to twenty-five graduates of the universities of Great Britain, the Empire, and the Commonwealth for two years' research at American universities. The ratio of British students to those from the Empire and Commonwealth was usually about five to one. So that, on that summer morning, there were twenty of us at most assembled in the London headquarters of the fund, a handsome Georgian house in Portman Square, which remained a graceful reminder of the Adam brothers until the bombs of the Luftwaffe provided the opportunity to re-create the square in cafeteria modern and lavatory tile. We were to be shepherded in a fleet of taxis to St. James's Palace, which contained within the facade of an Elizabethan fortress the Prince's small private residence, York House.

The Prince of Wales was the honorary chairman of the fellowships, and no doubt this annual ceremony of receiving the new Fellows and wishing them well was to him yet another of the endless tedious chores that hobble the days and nights of royalty. (After watching an American television show in which a cream puff of a blonde was proclaimed "Queen for a Day" and announced that her fondest fantasy was to enjoy the luxurious and carefree life of a monarch, I went through a year of the London *Times*'s court calendar and discovered that the Queen of England had had in all about thirty-odd days to herself and fewer evenings still.) Edward, as the Prince of Wales, had his titular duties toward hospitals, regiments, training ships, eisteddfods, memorial services, state visits, and the like; and long after the First War was over he felt a genuine obligation to the men he had seen in the trenches and voluntarily involved himself in veterans' organizations that took care of the permanently disabled. But he paid an extra price for his unique popularity in being drenched by a continuous blizzard of invitations from institutions both grand and trivial in every country of the Empire.

The small band of scientists, historians, English scholars, and such that bowled down St. James's Street were high on the waggishness with which young college types cover up their self-consciousness on state

occasions and, in this instance, their childlike awe at
the prospect of coming face to face with the legendary
Prince Charming. And here I ought to say something
about the wonder of that legend, even in that time of
depression and social restlessness. It was built on two
assets: a long tradition of royal respectability that
began with Queen Victoria and was entrenched in the
reign of George V; and the welcome relief that was
brought to the rigors of that tradition by personal
qualities, in the Prince, of charm and mischief.

ALMOST HALF A CENTURY AFTER THIS, for me, bright
and memorable morning, it is easy to wince at the
resounding hollowness of such ceremonial phrases as
"Emperor of India," "Defender of the Faith," "Queen
Mother," or even "Prince Charming." But in those
days, Buckingham Palace was the symbolic family
town house for nearly one-third of the earth. The
monarchy was still stage-lit with feudal trappings and
much indigenous and breathtaking theatrical ritual. It
would take forty years or so for the camera of the
muckraker to pull back and show in long shot—once
the Empire was lost—the tininess of the stage and the
still huge staff of courtiers, chamberlains, press
officers, private secretaries, ladies- and lords-in-
waiting who contributed to the illusion of power,
regality, and magic.

To be sure, in gamier days, the British monarchy
had been the butt of private gossip and public
cartoonists. Rowlandson had savagely caricatured the
love life of the Prince Regent, and when he died as
George IV, the London *Times* had appeared with an
editorial enclosed in deferential black borders that
began: "There can hardly be a wet eye in the kingdom
for this debauched monarch." Very late in her reign,

Queen Victoria and her son had been drawn by Max Beerbohm as comical and lugubrious figures. George V, the Prince's own father, had once been abused by a Labor Member of Parliament as "a German pork butcher." But these were fugitive darts tossed against the armor plate of Victorian respectability, a code that solidified through the long high noon of the imperial mother's reign. True, it was suspended briefly during the sybaritic interlude of Edward VII, what with the baccarat and divorce scandals, the occasional photograph of the King strolling with an unidentified lady at Cannes or driving to the races with an hourglass figure whom the bold and knowing would identify as Lily Langtry. But the code of respectability, and its collateral assumption of domestic purity in the Crown, had spread wide and deep throughout the nineteenth century and watered the nonconformist conscience of the rising middle class. It achieved its most effective public image, after the momentary distortions of the Edwardians, in George V.

All of us born at the beginning of his reign knew nothing for several decades about the Edwardian goings-on. We accepted, as children do, the existing mores and ethics, and they were the mores and ethics of good King George. It would have been as inconceivable in my childhood not to think of him as kindly, pious, and fatherly as it would have been in my youth to ask why the duchy of Cornwall provided a very large annual income for the Prince of Wales, or why the monarchy cost the taxpayers the $11 million a year that a Scottish Member of Parliament was to make such a rumpus about in 1975.

It was the historical good fortune of Edward, Prince of Wales, to be the principal beneficiary of this assumption of respectability. That it may also have been the spur to his downfall is another matter. So long as his father reigned, the Prince Charming legend was nurtured by gallant tales of the plucky little midshipman and by such widespread—and true—rumors that during the most murderous years of the war he had begged for, and been denied, the opportunity to go "up front" to the trenches. Even his peccadilloes were seen as delightful spasms of animal spirits in a virtuous and unshakable family: the usual material for good-humored gossip by the neighbors. It was pleasant to imagine the discomfiture of the old King when it came out that his son was keeping the burghers of Oxford awake with his ukulele. He was a brave horseman but kept falling off his horse, and the papers rustled with reports of the Queen's insistence that he should give up hunting. From time to time, the daughters of reigning European nobility descended on Windsor, and when such a one was a radiant Swedish Princess, the matrons of Britain twittered at the imminence of a royal wedding. But the Princess went away, and the matrons sighed. "He doesn't," said my puzzled father, "seem to be interested in girls at all." My mother, with a little more realism, ventured: "One day he'll be caught like all the rest of us."

But he went his dazzling way, as the world's most eligible—or, rather, most desirable—bachelor. And every other year or so, he was off on his mission as "the Empire's best salesman" (whatever that meant), and the papers and the newsreels excited applauding audiences with his flashing good looks, his almost childlike naturalness, and the vast surging crowds in India, Egypt, South Africa, America, Australia, Paris, wherever. In the only biography written at the time, an official and—it now appears—a fairly unctuous effort, by one Major F. E. Verney, an equerry, what does emerge is that as a roving ambassador he had a genuine wish to know about the lands he had to visit and the gorgeous range of human magnificoes and oddities who inhabited them. (An English friend of mine who was no great admirer of the Prince visited him for a weekend at Fort Belvedere and came back frankly astounded at "the consummate knowledge he revealed of every remote corner of the Empire as he showed off a wall of framed maps in his living room.") He may have had no enduring interest in elections, defense statistics, Arab kingdoms, or unemployment, but he always appeared concerned, and the statesmen, generals, sheikhs, and labor leaders were always on tap to instruct and surprise him. And his official duties, though unabated into his forties, provided both a discipline and a curiosity shop that kept him lively and inquisitive.

IN 1932, HE WAS THIRTY-EIGHT, and while he was a little old for a Prince Charming, the public picture of him had not dimmed. It was even sharpened by tart revelations about his personal habits that upset nobody but the conservative upper classes. He no longer rode to hounds. There were fewer overseas tours. He stayed at home most of the time, and when he was not photographed opening a British Legion outpost or christening a ship, he was shown by day in the company of jockeys or famous golfers, and by night, trig but slightly pouch-eyed, with various Mayfair "honorables" in West End clubs. There were well-circulated rumors of spats with his father about the dashing, rather loud checks he wore, and about his nighttime addiction to jazz. None of this—though it had the old guard hissing that they were about to inherit a "cad" for a king—did him any harm with the mass of the people. It certainly did not lessen the awe with which our company of university graduates approached him, as we went through the gateway of St. James's Palace and were saluted by a guard right out of *Iolanthe*. To us—to those of us in particular from Oxford and Cambridge who affected the sophisticated fatigue fashionable in the early thirties—the Prince's little social rebellions were a heartening sign that he was "one of the lads" who would take the starch out of royal protocol and move the monarchy, when his time came, into the twentieth century.

We were led into a large reception room and greeted with such confident urbanity by three aides, or gentlemen-in-waiting, that whatever poise we had mustered for the occasion was reduced to the timidity of a country cousin being presented with his first wine list. Between the reception room and the Prince's apartments there were two high doors encrusted with gilt and bearing the emblem of the fleur-de-lis. (If they did not, this trick of memory will only go to confirm my romantic prejudice in his favor.) The aides occasionally glanced at wristwatches and got off such predictable Wodehouseisms as: "Strordnry! Never known him not to be on the dot," or, "Be along presently, I'm quite shaw—*do* sit down." They sought to put us at our ease with expert small talk about the quick-blooming summer and other trivia.

There was a sudden choirboy babble from the inner room which, if it had been heard more often on the radio, would have been instantly recognizable as the Prince's voice. Although we had never heard it, we guessed at its owner and adjusted our neckties in tribute. I recall shooting a cuff myself, since on the advice of an undergraduate friend of mine, a young man of deafening poise and the son of a distinguished West End actor, I had acquired his tailor and encased myself, for this royal occasion, in a brand-new double-breasted houndstooth suit. When the two doors opened and the Prince came in, I was amazed and comforted to see that he was wearing a suit of the identical material and cut. This happy coincidence, on the snobbish Oxbridge scorecard of the day, put me one up with one hole to play.

The first thought was how much older he seemed than his pictures. The second that he was surprisingly nervous, not an unattractive trait because it suggested that he had not grown blasé from the wealth of such ceremonies he had had to put up with, and that every encounter with a stranger was a human occasion. And so it seemed to be. We were ushered into a file and presented to him one by one, and I noticed that he looked every Fellow in the eye and inquired after his specialty. The much-advertised charm was undoubtedly present. The bags under the eyes, which we might have been inclined to attribute to those late nights with the girls of Mayfair, could also be ascribed to the Hanoverian or Saxe Coburg—or, after 1916, the Windsor—blood strain. Edward VII had the same bulging, mournful stare, and so did King George. Still, his world-weary look was not enlivened by listening to what one man was going to do in physics and another in molecular chemistry. The man immediately in front of me was going to the West Coast, to Pacific Grove I think, to learn how to rehabilitate the English oyster beds that had been damaged by the submarine warfare of the comparatively recent war. This was just the sort of thing that the Prince liked to find out about, and he was roused by this peculiar specialty.

Then it was my turn. The Prince had turned to one of his gentlemen for some casual remark, and when he turned back, he looked up and said in a startled tone, "My God, my brother!" I hope it doesn't sound conceited for me to say that this line surprised me less than the others standing round, for I had been kidded for years by my friends because of a fancied resemblance to the Prince's youngest brother, Prince George, later the Duke of Kent. But, for all its ridiculous triviality, it was a moment of odd intimacy. (He made the same remark, with the same air of surprise, on three subsequent occasions.) He at once said that I ought to forgive him but had anyone ever told me, etc., and I said that they had, but coming from you, sir, etc., etc. And what was my "field" of study? (I noticed then how strange that he should use what in those days was an exotic Americanism. He had already met Mrs. Simpson, but for several years before he met her he had moved in an Anglo-American circle. I remember how, four years later, when he made his first radio talk as King, following the custom of his father, he said something about the marvel of "the radio," and an old Englishman I was listening with exploded in disgust at the solecism and shouted, "It's those Americans he goes with." Years ago, however, the British abandoned "the wireless" and succumbed to the radio.)

I had been awarded my fellowship to study American theater direction. The committee of award was taking a risk in appointing a Fellow in a "field" so unacademic, and I was told later that its chairman, Lord Halifax, felt so more than most but agreed to my appointment on the grounds that he was a North Countryman and so was I and "on the whole, we are the most reliable types."

At the mention of theater, the Prince's eyes bulged more than usual. Visions—I felt sure—of the Ziegfeld and Vanities choruses floated before him. He wanted to know what the Americans had to teach about directing plays that "our own fellahs" didn't know, and he was willing, even eager, to believe that there was a great deal. Would I, he asked, tugging at his cuffs and

59

lowering his voice a little, expect to direct musicals? It was a shocking suggestion to an earnest student who had spent a summer with the German Volksbühne and who was convinced that what the English theater needed was less attention to playwrights and more to the military manipulation of actors on the stage, in accordance with the dictatorial methods of Piscator and Meyerhold. I wish now I had had the wit, or the mischief, to say "of course." (Two years later, I seized the opportunity to direct the ancient Hasty Pudding Club of Harvard in its annual knobbly-kneed musical.) The Prince drooped visibly, and rightly, at my earnest exposition of the superior discipline of the German and American directors, and after a little exchange about the fact that American "director" then meant English "producer," I moved on.

For the next two years, while I was in America, I saw the Prince of Wales, like almost everybody and everything else in Britain, through the flip headlines of the American tabloids and the Homeric compound adjectives of *Time* ("Britain's moose-tall ambassador, Sir Ronald Lindsay") as part of a newly discovered Gilbert and Sullivan operetta. Against a faintly sketched background of England's money troubles, her "distressed areas," her untroubled view of Hitler, the royal family loomed larger than it had at home and almost as large as the horror-movie menace of the Loch Ness Monster.

As a student visitor rollicking in the Depression-proof subsidy of a well-paid fellowship, I certainly had other things on my mind than the British monarchy, which now—through American spectacles—seemed impressive but quaint. The only time I remember its ever coming up was on a visit to Vancouver to pay a courtesy call on a judge who was a relation of an old college friend. The Canadian family seemed remarkably anxious for news of the King, as if I were some kind of envoy, but when, over tea, I used the undergraduate's normal facetious word and said something like "I don't think George would take that very well," the family reacted to this thunderclap of tastelessness by getting rid of me in a hurry. Evidently, distance lends more things than enchantment, including an obligation to revere, at 6000 miles, what on the home ground is taken for granted.

Once I was back in England, it was never possible again to look on the monarchy in the old respectful but offhand way. But if I could now muster all the usual republican arguments, I also saw that it carried a blessing or two that had never crossed my mind. After a two-year exposure to the "society" pages of big-city and small-town newspapers, it did seem that the presence up there of one towering social arbiter made all the lower scrambles for status useless. When there is a King and Queen, there is no point in trying to be a Du Pont or a thirties version of Jackie Onassis.

In 1935, I was approached, on behalf of the National Broadcasting Company, by a very suave and affable American to broadcast a weekly *London Letter* to the United States. The gentleman was Frederick Bate, a Chicago expatriate who in the twenties had dabbled in painting but dabbled more effectively in the Anglo-American social crowd that held court in Paris and on the Riviera. He was now the chief European representative of NBC—so far as I could see, the only one. Those were the wildcat days of transatlantic broadcasting, and looking back on him now, after forty years' familiarity with American broadcasting, I can only say that Fred Bate was a freak and a welcome one, as unlike a network executive as it was possible to be. He was courtly, modest, good-natured, the apotheosis of savoir faire and New World courtesy. We became close friends, and after my regular Sunday evening broadcast, from a studio hired from the British Broadcasting Corporation, we retreated together to dinner either at his house or at a favorite restaurant on Jermyn Street. Bate had too much social ease to curry favors or drop names, but it soon came out that he was an intimate of the Prince of Wales, and after January, 1936, therefore of the King. Bate shed no gossip and never breathed a confidence. But on many a Friday afternoon or Saturday morning he would begin to watch the time, finally excusing himself to head for a weekend at Fort Belvedere, which was the sanctuary of the Prince's private Anglo-American café society.

In the summer of 1935, I was putting on, for the BBC, a series of radio feature programs called *The American Half-Hour*, which hoped to convey to the benighted British the enlightenment of a tour of the United States. It began with a program on New York, and one of its entertaining aims was to give the sense of a Broadway first night. To do this on radio, all you need is a bright idea or two, a phonograph record, a sound-effect disc of a theater audience, and an actor or two to play the members of the theater party. I employed Ben Welden, an American actor working in London, as the American host, and Robert Speaight as the English visitor who was going to be instructed and amazed from coast to coast. (A small but needling point I wanted to make to the nation of shopkeepers was that in American theaters, the programs were free.) The only thing I lacked was the phonograph record of Ethel Merman singing "You're the Top" from the hit we wanted to simulate: *Anything Goes*. The show had not yet arrived in England, but the London impresario who owned the rights was eventually prevailed upon to let the hit song have a single promotional fling over our program. But where to find a bootlegged copy of the record? In such fixes, Bate was always the man. He gave me an address in Bryanston Court, an apartment house, and told me that at six o'clock precisely on such a day, a lady would be waiting in such and such a flat to lend me her precious contraband. I went there, was shown in by a maid, and waited in a discreetly sumptuous sitting room. Presently there appeared a small middle-aged brunette, clipping on the earring that would give the last touch of elegance to an impeccable production. She had coiled braids pinned above her ears, darting blue-black eyes, and a determined square jaw. She also had a mid-Atlantic accent grafted on a faint Southern base. She extended to me the brief courtesy of a drink chased with enthusiastic small talk about the talents of Cole Porter and the endearing brashness of Ethel Merman. Then she handed me the record and I was on my way out. For another year or more, I should have had to make an effort to recall her name from this hasty encounter. She was a Mrs. Simpson.

I saw her once again. My mother had come down from the North to visit us in London, and we took her to the opening night of the Astaire-Rogers movie musical *Top Hat*. We sat in the third row of the dress circle, and when the film was already well along, a man and woman came out of the darkness and took the two seats immediately in front of us. He was in a dinner jacket, and as he turned toward his companion and fiddled with his tie, his profile against the blazing white of the lower half of the screen—the boyish arc of the head, the brushed-up forelock, the perky little nose and wistful pop eyes—was unmistakably that of the Prince of Wales. It was the thrill of my mother's life.

They were in bubbling spirits, still playing out some dinnertime joke, and the people nearby—peering around to spot the source of this nuisance, and failing—shushed them into silence. The Prince paid little attention to the movie, chuckling to himself occasionally with no obvious provocation from what was going on on the screen, and from time to time he heaved a sigh as light as a kitten's and rested his head on the lady's gleaming shoulder. Several times, she roused him with a giggle. When the film was over and the lights went up, the orchestra went into the drum-roll that announces the national anthem. Everybody stood up, and the Prince, his chest out in the sergeant major's prescribed stance, his elbows braced akimbo, his body weaving very slightly, could be seen by everybody for who he was. For the first time in my mother's life, the awful suspicion entered her mind that the Prince might not be a virgin. (My father held a similar touching view of the chastity of *his* hero, David Lloyd George, and luckily didn't live long enough to lose it.)

This simple scene brought me a long way—it was only ten years—from my first sight of the Prince, when he came up to Cleveleys, a small town on the Lancashire coast, to open a convalescent home for miners, and stood there in a gusty wind coming in from the Irish sea, the wings of his unreal golden hair fluttering around his ears, his pink face properly grave as he begged us to remember what we all owed to the men who went down into the earth for all our sakes.

Now, in 1935, in the year before his father died, he seemed to be very much on the town, in a discreet way. But once he was King, his public appearances became obviously and exclusively ceremonial. The rumors that he was going to find his intimacy with Mrs. Simpson an embarrassment as King never passed beyond the confines of the Cabinet and the very small circle of the Mayfair and Belgravia *haut monde*. His first appearances as King were exemplary. The short speech he addressed to the assembled Privy Councillors was admiringly reported: "When my father stood here twenty-six years ago, he declared that one of the objects of his life would be to uphold constitutional government. In this I am determined to follow in my father's footsteps and to work as he did throughout his life for the happiness and welfare of my subjects. I place my reliance upon the loyalty and affection of my peoples throughout the Empire, and upon the wisdom of their Parliaments, to support me in this heavy task, and I pray God will guide me to perform it." Few words he ever spoke in public thereafter were to carry in retrospect so many ironies.

However, he at once gave the most gallant sign of respect for the dead King. A few minutes after midnight, of the day on which a continuous file of people had passed by the coffin in Westminster Hall, four men in resplendent uniforms appeared, on the new King's orders, and stood around the catafalque. They were the four royal brothers, including the King himself. On the day of the funeral, they strode together through London, accompanying the body to San-dringham, and, following the procession, I was struck by one detail. The King's face was frozen in a bleak, immobile expression, but his jaw muscles flexed in rhythm as if to a metronome. A little later in the year, he was returning on horseback from presenting the colors to three Guards regiments. As he was riding up Constitution Hill on a gray day a man broke through the police line, there was a scuffle, and a revolver clattered across the pavement and skittered between the hooves of the King's horse. If it was not an assassination attempt, it was as close to one as made no matter. The King barely reined in his horse, looked straight ahead with his stony, mournful expression, and rode on. This, too, brought splendid reassurance to any citizens who had had doubts about the transformation of a playboy into a worthy King.

He was seen now only on formal occasions, or lifting his hat from inside a closed car, sliding through the gray London days or appearing briefly to surprise bystanders and then vanishing into the fog of the London nights.

Some of the remoteness of that time, which is preserved in memory with the period quality of an old daguerreotype, is undoubtedly due to the dramatic change in the literal atmosphere of London between the first half of the century and the second. The gloom of the events of December, 1936, was intensified by the pathetic fallacy, dear to authors of detective stories, of the dank London winter and its enshrouding fogs. To anyone who knew London well before the 1960s, it is today an unrecognizably clean, bright city. The change was heralded in 1956, when with very little fanfare Parliament passed a Clean Air Act. At a time when airline passengers in the United States were learning to accept as a fact of life a descent into the yellow veil of smog that lay increasingly over New York and Los Angeles, the Greater London Council (as it is now called) systematically banished the burning of soft coal and all other smoky fuels, and by 1970 every metropolitan borough had been fumigated. Since the Londoner, like the vast majority of Britons, had until then heated his little castle with a bituminous-coal fire, the restriction on its noxious smoke alone gave London for the first time in memory clean air, undreamed-of-nighttime vistas, and a million cold chimney pots as useless reminders of a century and a half of industrial smog.

But in the 1930s and beyond the second quarter of the century there was another London, now encapsulated for the young only in the large body of English fiction that stretches from the early Dickens to the early Graham Greene. It is the London whose winter evenings Hollywood loved to re-create with offstage machines pumping clouds of fog onto the silhouettes of Basil Rathbone and Nigel Bruce as they strode off for the eight twenty-nine from Paddington in pursuit of some horrific mischief in the West Country—a London that on the fairest days glimmered with a rusty light and by night simmered in a stew of gray mist through which such a landmark as the Tower or the Houses of Parliament loomed up like the prow of an oncoming liner.

Tuesday, the first of December, 1936, ended in such an evening, though one strangely aglow on the southeastern horizon with the still-burning inferno of the old Crystal Palace, the glass-and-iron masterpiece of Victorian festival architecture in whose charred remains clergymen, reporters, and other amateur sociologists were soon to recognize an omen of the collapse of the Victorian ideals of duty and domestic tranquillity. That evening, the English-Speaking Union was holding, in its restored mid-eighteenth-century mansion in Mayfair, the first meeting of a newly appointed Research and Discussion Committee. It had called together a dozen eminent and obscure men who had, one way or another, an interest in improving the British view of the United States. In the chair was a handsome silver-haired snapdragon of a Scotsman in his early fifties—Sir Frederick Whyte, who could be expected to keep the discussion on a practical, unsentimental level. He had been for five years the President of the Legislative Assembly of India and subsequently the chief political adviser to the national government of China, had picked up a garland of honorary degrees after much travel in the United States, and was to become, during the Second

67

World War, the head of the American Division of the Ministry of Information.

There was no discernible ideological bias among the group sitting round a long oval table. We were a mixed lot. A soldier. A lawyer. A conservative Member of Parliament. An American newspaper correspondent. An academic or two. An English journalist, a Harvard roommate of mine during our tenure of a Commonwealth Fellowship. David Low, the cartoonist. And Kingsley Martin, the editor of the leftist *New Statesman*. Martin was one of those ferocious democrats who insist on dominating any open discussion, but I can't be sure now whether it was this trait or his extraordinarily baleful appearance that makes him, forty years later, stand out in my memory like a gorgon at a garden party. He had enormous brown eyes, like hyperthyroid marbles, which rolled across a sallow face that appeared to be in the last stages of hepatitis. He was, I recall, buoyant with his accustomed gloom, for he was a man devoted to catastrophe, and just then he had a lot of it to revel in: the siege of Madrid by Franco's forces, Hitler's assumption of the Rhineland, the League of Nations' resigned acquiescence in Mussolini's conquest of Ethiopia.

All these things were touched on, but Sir Frederick kept begging Martin to dismount from his hobbyhorse in order to bring the meeting back to the purpose it had been called for: to suggest ways of adjusting the British stereotypes of America in the 1920s to the crusading, the then almost heroic, figure of Roosevelt and the phenomenon of the New Deal. What is remarkable now about the free-ranging agenda of this meeting is that these informed and articulate men, drinking amiably together, at no time brought up the apocalyptic domestic events of the previous two weeks, with which all contemporary historians confidently begin their account of the ten days that shook the British Empire and ended in the first voluntary abdication of a British King.

Several of us there had been in America that summer and been startled by reams of sober and gossipy speculation about the dire consequences of a royal episode that no more than a few hundred Britons at most had ever heard of—namely, the King's affair with Mrs. Simpson. Two weeks before that meeting, the Labor MP Ellen Wilkinson had risen in the House of Commons to ask the President of the Board of Trade why two American magazines "of the highest repute" (she was talking about *Time* and *News Review*) had had "two and sometimes three pages torn out" of the copies sold in Britain. "Can he say," she had asked, "what is this thing the British public are not allowed to know?" Even to the sitting Commons, there was probably no irony in this artless question. The Minister said it was not the business of his department, and the question was put down for a later reply by the Home Secretary, whose views, if any, were shortly over-whelmed by events. After this brief emergence of an inquisitive periscope, Parliament and the press submerged again. Yet, that same day, a democratic Congressman from Wisconsin had announced that he would introduce a resolution asking President Roosevelt to forbid American ambassadors and any other American officials to attend the coronation of a King "who proposed marriage to an American divorcee."

Beginning that day—the seventeenth of November—*The New York Times* carried regular front-page dispatches on what it guessed was inevitably to be a British constitutional crisis. On the twenty-sixth, it reported a meeting at Buckingham Palace between the

King and Prime Minister Stanley Baldwin at which, the *Times* correctly inferred, the King had threatened to abdicate. (The British press recorded the audience in a couple of lines as a regulation courtesy visit.) On the twenty-eighth, the *Times* reported at length an emergency Cabinet meeting, held to discuss the King's personal problem and his apparently implacable decision to abdicate. (The British papers headlined "an emergency" but chose to assume it was about Britain's decision to stay neutral in the Spanish Civil War.)

On the morning of our meeting, *The New York Times* frontpaged an assurance by Clement Attlee, the leader of the parliamentary opposition, that the Labor Party would not take any political advantage of the impasse with the King. None of this appeared by even the subtlest indirection in the British press, which had yielded to a firm nudge from the Newspaper Proprietors' Association to suppress all mention of the King's affair. The crisis, in fact, was beyond retrieval, and the King was weighing his final decision, before a British journal ever printed the name of Mrs. Simpson except as an unidentified palace guest in the *Court Circulars* and later on as the plaintiff in an obscure divorce case heard in a court in the provinces.

(I had read all the *New York Times* dispatches— usually about a week after their publication—because I was a good friend of Ferdinand Kuhn, Jr., the head of *The New York Times*'s London bureau, a first-rate reporter and an American with an uncommonly sensitive feel for parliamentary procedure and morale. Before the dam broke, he was saying quietly that he saw no alternative to abdication. And when we were all bending against the storm, he said as much to a Foreign Office acquaintance. "My dear Kuhn," the man countered, "English Kings don't abdicate.")

It came out later that Kingsley Martin, days before our meeting, had written and sent to the palace for the King's approval (a very odd journalistic gesture in a knowledgeable Englishman) a long editorial in which he rent the veil from the whole affair and took the King's side. Whether or not palace intermediaries ever permitted it to reach the King, the approval never came. Martin, that smoggy December night, was hot for British intervention in Spain—on the Republican side—and for a campaign to enlist Roosevelt's aid against Franco.

Yet we all leaned back there, sitting on a charge of dynamite. We were aware of it. We were concerned. We were tactful. And we were mum. Indeed, by about ten o'clock, when the drinks had mellowed the talk, David Low was being urged to discover some more contemporary symbol than the typical American of his cartoons—a moon-faced man with horn-rimmed spectacles and belted trousers hitched high above his ankles. Low facetiously protested that national stereotypes are what the reader is looking for and, anyway, take decades to die. But he promised to reform "in the unlikely event that horn-rimmed glasses and turned-down collars worn with dinner jackets ever catch on in this country." (They caught on within a year or two. With the King they had already caught on.)

A knock came on the door, and a prune-faced butler glided to the chairman's side and announced, "There is a telephone call from New York for Mr. Cooke."

It is hard today to convey the sinister prestige implicit in such a line at such a time. Long before the transatlantic cable, when the radio circuits had to go from New York to exotic places like Tangier, telephone calls between London and the United States were placed only by such as the Rockefellers,

71

Presidents of the United States, and export-import millionaires. The meeting was chilled into silence by the news that I was wanted on the phone, and Sir Fredrick gave me an alarmed but kindly look as if I, a young film critic with a known bee in my bonnet about the United States, had been suddenly unmasked as an informer. Flushed with an embarrasssment heavily tinged with self-importance, I excused myself and was taken into an adjoining office.

The faint but excited voice was that of Fred Bate, a victim of an irony that the NBC big shots could only thrash over in impotent rage. Here was Bate, a close friend of the King, presumably with a personal pipeline to Fort Belvedere, who now had the ill luck—at that juncture—to find himself for the first time in many years on a holiday in his native land, and stranded, for in those days the fastest way to England, by ship, took five days. My regular broadcast to America was done on Sundays. Today was Tuesday. Bate's excited little speech was feverish to the point of delirium, a frightening departure from his invariable urbanity. Some station in Schenectady had announced that the King would probably abdicate. What in God's name did Schenectady know, and why bring up the matter at all, since Britons had never heard of Mrs. Simpson? Because, Bate panted, the Bishop of Bradford had broken the voluntary censorship and castigated the King that very day. The American papers were full of it. NBC had booked a circuit with the BBC for a quarter to midnight. It was "vital" I should get to Broadcasting House, do a five-minute talk, six minutes, anything, and finish before midnight. (What was "vital" was NBC's knowledge that Bate's alert London rival, Cesar Searchinger of CBS, had booked a midnight circuit.) Bate went on breathlessly. They would break into any program on the air. Nothing would be believed in America from now on except what came from London. Be there. Please! Good boy.

Rattled by the naiveté of this outburst, I said I would do the best I could and try to report "the reaction" from the capital city, which so far knew nothing to react to. I collected my old Harvard friend, who was on the editorial staff of the *News Chronicle*, and we drove off to Fleet Street. There we found his newsroom buzzing with the rumor that the Yorkshire dailies were about to break out in a rash of editorials based upon what the Bishop of Bradford had said in a speech before a diocesan conference at Bradford. They all took it for granted that in two sentences Bishop Blunt had brought into the open at last the stifled affair with Mrs. Simpson and, living up to his name, had roundly lamented the King's need of grace: "We hope that he is aware of this need. Some of us wish that he gave more positive signs of that awareness." Acting on the same assumption, the *News Chronicle* itself had prepared an editorial, directing the bishop's censure at its obvious object. We took a smudgy galley of this piece in a taxi to Broadcasting House. Arrived in a small third-floor studio, I saw that only five minutes remained before the New York circuit would open. I was greeted by one of the regular BBC news announcers, always, in those days, trenchant upper-middle-class types. This one was a retired major with an arrogant county manner. I quickly parried his rather peremptory demands to know what this was all about. He ducked into the control room, the red light glowed on, and I ad-libbed as best I could, decrying the mere thought of abdication, recounting for a knowing American audience the amazing sustained silence of the British press, and hoping that the bishop knew what he was doing in breaking it.

The moment the red light went off, the announcer

bounded in and stood before me trembling with anger. He braced himself like a headmaster about to pronounce the expulsion of a senior prefect caught in an unspeakably loathsome crime. Blue with rage, and flexing his jaw muscles like pistons, he said very deliberately, "I have *never* heard anything like it. It is *absolutely monstrous* that an Englishman should use a BBC circuit to denigrate His Majesty the King before a foreign audience. You may be *quite* sure that I shall report this to my superiors." And he whisked out.

Nothing more was heard of this threat, and no wonder. Within forty-eight hours, every London daily had rocketing headlines about the King and his mistress. Six North Country papers pried open the floodgates next morning and after them came the deluge. Bishop Blunt, it turned out, was the most innocent of dam busters. His speech had protested the suggestion of a famous progressive bishop that the clergymen of the free churches (the nonconformists) should be invited to participate in the coronation service. To Bishop Blunt, this amounted to a radical call for the disestablishment of the Church of England. He had spoken with great gravity about the sacredness of the coronation ceremony, committing the monarch to a holy union with his people under God. In a sighing afterthought, he had lamented the King's indifference to churchgoing, and then uttered his two regretful sentences about the King's insufficient grace. When he was asked about it, it was revealed that he, too, had never heard of Mrs. Simpson.

For the next ten days the British press behaved like a Sunday school teacher who, caught out in some tiny offense, assumes that it must be the first irrevocable step toward damnation and so had better go the whole way down the primrose path. Editors who had been splenetic at the suggestion that they might risk a hint of the forbidden subject now wrote about nothing else. The London papers added two extra evening editions. The American press and the radio networks, vindicated beyond their guiltiest dreams of *lèse majesté*, wallowed in what H.L. Mencken called "the greatest story since the Crucifixion."

The telephone calls from Bate in New York were now as frequent and frantic as those of a movie star separated from his latest doxy. Whereas the Columbia Broadcasting System decided to enlarge on the agency dispatches from London, and the coverage of its own man, with nightly talks by such distinguished Britons as H. G. Wells and Harold Nicolson (performing without fear of an outraged announcer), NBC chose to stay with me alone, and set up circuits six and seven times a day. I found myself putting New York to bed at four in the morning London time, doing the same for California three hours later, then waking New York at our noon, the Mountain States at two, California at three, and so on. This grueling routine brought me down for several days with an infection that was roaming around London, but the alert Bate was not to be put off by a low-grade fever. He had the British Post Office set up a line to my house and install a microphone in my living room, into which I padded from my bed every two hours or so to deliver the next installment of a running story that amounted, by the time it was all over, to about 400,000 words. (It remains my record for a ten-day stint.)

Luckily, just before I fell ill, I had a call from a young American at Oxford, the younger brother of one of my first American friends. This enthusiastic Rhodes Scholar was coming to London, and he jumped at the offer of bed and board in exchange for his services as a legman feeding both the wild and the responsible talk of the town to a housebound correspondent. Every day, the blond, bespectacled twenty-year-old dashed between the pubs and the clubs, including rallies of the Communists and of Oswald Mosley's fascist Blackshirts, both of whom agreed, for once, that the King was a sorry victim of what we then called the System. My eager legman infiltrated the small crowds outside 10 Downing Street and the large crowds swarming around the palace, and he was plainly agog to find himself even peripherally engaged in the royal crisis. Thirty years later, he was to become more than an observer of great events. He was to conduct them, at the elbow of the President of the United States. His name was Walt W. Rostow.

By the tenth of December it was all over. In the morning, the King signed the instrument of abdication. In the afternoon, the Prime Minister rose in an unforgettable session of the Commons to give the simplest account of his meetings, his "I said to the King...the King told me" falling like tolling bells in the graveyard silence of the House. On the eleventh, an order of the new King quietly resolved a fuss of protocol over how the ex-King should be introduced for his broadcast speech to the nation. As "His Royal Highness Prince Edward," he gave his farewell talk, went to the royal lodge at Windsor, to say good-bye to his mother, his sister, and his three brothers, and then drove off to Portsmouth to go aboard a waiting destroyer. At two in the morning of the twelfth, the *Fury* slid into a thick Channel fog. Its passenger was bound for Boulogne and thirty-five years of exile. Three days later, *The New York Times*'s epilogue on the whole affair was a single-column dispatch headlined "Parliament Hears Pledge by George to Duty and Honor."

In the intervening forty-one years, all this has been drastically reduced, in several popular histories, to a simple or a cruel conflict between a headstrong, romantic King and a bigoted Establishment led by Baldwin and the archbishop of Canterbury, and it has been made the subject of special pleading, disguised as reluctant but true confessions, by interested parties—not least by the Duke of Windsor in *A King's Story* and the Duchess in *The Heart Has Its Reasons*. Not until Frances Donaldson published her biography *Edward VIII* were we given a definitive life so informed with hitherto unpublished and telling intimacies as to offer the continuous shock of discovering a new story and an unknown King.

We never knew, in the Prince Charming era of the Empire tours, that when the parades were all over and the bunting was down, he was a moody man and a defiant son who never did enough or never did it the right way (witness his flashy clothes and his too informal approach to rajahs and kings) to suit his father. It took, indeed, nearly forty years after the abdication for us to modify at all our picture of his father. Until the last five years or so, biographers of living British royalty were so habituated to the *lèse majesté* taboo that they went into a kind of trance more effective as an inhibiting leash than any Official Secrets Act. And even so acute an observer of people and things as Harold Nicolson, writing his life of George V in the 1950s, could produce nothing better than an official biography that very rarely goes beyond the reverent contemplation of a godhead. Out of it emerges a simply more persuasive image of the kindly, sensible old monarch, of much natural dignity, with more political savvy than you might give him credit for, and with a warming gift of sympathy for one or two people beyond his ken, as witness his friendship with J. H. Thomas, the homespun, aitchless railway union leader who had left school at the age of ten. The press was

similarly hypnotized by long habit into seeing not only
no evil but no idiosyncrasy in the royal family, hearing
none and reporting none. We knew little of the Prince's
domestic upbringing, next to nothing about his
miserably sparse education, and nothing at all about
good King George's social bigotry, his abysmal—
almost proud—ignorance of the arts, letters, sciences
of the past and present, and his hysterical strictness
with his sons ("I was frightened of my father, and I am
damn well going to see to it that my children are
frightened of me"). Nor did we ever hear, until 1972,
the astonishing remark made to Prime Minister
Baldwin by King George, after the Simpson affair had
begun to trouble him: "After I am dead, the boy will
ruin himself in twelve months." Nobody before Lady
Donaldson had access, or chose to have access, to such
unexampled wealth of official documents and records,
from the Foreign Office and the India Office to papers,
private letters, notes of conversations, and the like
contributed by almost everyone who was close to the
former Prince, King, and Duke of Windsor. They
range all the way from reminiscences by his cousin Earl
Mountbatten to Baldwin's niece, from aides, brother
officers, old companions to the most faithful of his
mistresses. Most disturbing of all, there are the
captured German documents which relate to the Nazis'
eagerness to keep the exiled Edward in Spain as a
potential puppet king after their intended conquest of
Europe, a prospect which—there is little doubt—
sporadically appealed to Edward throughout the time
of the Nazis' triumphs. It requires a frightful but
sobering reappraisal of the Prince Charming character
to see poor Windsor, during the aimless limbo period
in Austria, France, and Spain, waiting guiltily for
Hitler's call, like a character in a Hitchcock or Fritz

Lang movie, but turning, down the years, only into a desiccated Graham Greene character.

One sees also with regretful clarity, now, how the incessant hectoring of George V spurred the son to mobilize the genes of his grandfather, Edward VII, and sent him off at twilight in pursuit of wealthy playgirls, congenial Army and Navy buddies, international socialites, and the midnight-to-dawn amusements of what came later to be called the jet set. And that led to Mrs. Simpson. Shortly after he met her, he abruptly refused all telephone calls from the mistress he had seen almost every day he was in London for seventeen years. He became, as his favorite and affectionate brother, Prince George, said, "besotted with infatuation." And that led to the overwhelming event of his life: the abdication.

What has been muffled, or oversimplified, it seems to me, in all the writing about it to this day is the force of the constitutional issue posed by the possible alternatives to abdication. If the conflict had been resolved in any other way, it would probably have led to a popular uprising in Britain and to debates so destructive in the Dominion Parliaments that the day of their secession would have been hastened. And here it may be well to summarize the issue, especially for Americans who, accustomed to a Constitution you can touch and see, tend to assume that the British Constitution, being mostly unwritten, is a rhetorical abstraction, a shadow without substance. Whereas in the United States the Constitution is a written document intended to be construed *as law*, in the last resort by the United States Supreme Court, the British Constitution (beginning with the Magna Carta) is a vast body of statutes, many of them written, of declarations, common law principles and precedents, which define the *power of the people*, through Parliament, *against* the power of the monarchy.

It is not, for instance, illegal for a Prime Minister to stay in office after a vote of "no confidence" registered by the House of Commons. But it is unconstitutional. And when the departing Prime Minister then goes to the palace to ask the King to dissolve Parliament, there is nothing in the law to require the King to do so. But in the last hundred years no sovereign has dared to flout the constitutional custom. In law, too, the marriage of a British sovereign is like any other. But the constitutional rule—which it took the English Revolution of 1688 to establish—is that in any conflict of power, the Parliament is above the King and he must accept the advice of his Ministers on everything that affects public policy and the public interest. (Since the "public interest"—not the public curiosity—in a royal marriage can fairly be represented only by the majority opinion of the House of Commons, this provision was crucial in the decision to let the King go.)

A general understanding of this historic rule, even some vigorous public argument about it, might have cleared the ground on which the King, the Parliament, and the people could have taken their stand. But the great mischief was done by the newspaper proprietors. Their voluntary suppression of all news about the King and his affair deprived the people, and great numbers of public men and women, including probably a majority of the House of Commons, of any relevant knowledge about the constitutional crisis when it broke on them like a hurricane. They were all awash in a roaring storm, grabbing at futile props to their public status, their self-esteem, and their romantic or moral view of the monarchy. They had only a few days in which to reexamine a radical conflict of power that had taken several centuries of English history to resolve in favor of the people's sovereignty.

The first effort of some Members of Parliament who wanted to help the King at all costs was to cite the Royal Marriages Act of 1772 as clear proof that the King alone had final veto power on the choice of a royal bride. This was, at the least, a perverse misreading of an act passed after two eighteenth-century dukes (Cumberland and Gloucester) had contracted marriages of which the King (George III) had disapproved. The act required the King's consent to all marriages of his descendants, but if they persisted in their marital intention, they must wait a year and then, on notice being given to the Privy Council, the marriage would be valid, "except both Houses of Parliament ... shall declare their disapprobation." Even by this act, Parliament retained its veto power.

The 1772 Royal Marriages Act did not, in hard fact, apply at all, since—as Baldwin reminded the House in his first public statement—"the King himself requires no consent from any other authority to make his marriage legal." The sticking point was the Cabinet's refusal to approve, not the marriage, but a marriage in which Mrs. Simpson, as Baldwin put it, "necessarily becomes Queen [and therefore] enjoys all the status, rights, and privileges which both by positive law and by [constitutional] custom attach to that position." And, passing down from the Cabinet, that would leave the approval or "disapprobation" to Parliament (and not only to the British Parliament, as we shall see).

Baldwin had, of course, acquainted the King early on of the Cabinet's "disapprobation." The King, after much lonely agonizing and confusing advice from friends and would-be Wolseys, therefore proposed—at the suggestion of Esmond Harmsworth, the son of

Lord Rothermere, proprietor of the *Daily Mail*—that Parliament should pass a law approving Mrs. Simpson as his consort but depriving her of the "status, rights and privileges" of a Queen. This would have been a morganatic marriage, an institution invented by ingenious German princes as a device for bypassing the inflexible caste system of the old and various German royal houses.

But, as the English editor J. A. Spender was alone in pointing out late in December, 1936, "The British royal house is not a caste, and there is no legal or Constitutional restriction on the choice of wives by its members." (Both the present Duke of Gloucester and his father married commoners. More to the point, so did Edward's successor, George VI, whose widow is the present Queen's mother.) The King himself was at first baffled by the morganatic proposal and thought it "strange and almost inhuman," and his legal adviser, Walter Monckton, KC, told him that the chances of passage of such a law were at best "dubious." But Mrs. Simpson later recalled his having said, "I'll try anything in the spot I'm in now."

What, however, he was fatally up against was not, except at the beginning, the British Cabinet's distaste for Mrs. Simpson as Queen or consort but that so-called nonconformist conscience, which throughout the nineteenth century had given rise first to a reforming Liberal Party, then to a powerful labor movement, and had been a rugged force in the settling of the Dominions. It can be seen now that the King's number was up once it became plain that the British Labor Party in Parliament shared the "disapprobation" of the Cabinet. In the end, it was the resistance of the nonconformist conscience in the Dominions that finished him. He was doomed by the most recent rule of the Constitution—the very explicitly written Statute of Westminster, which in 1931 declared that "any alteration in the law touching the Succession of the Throne or the Royal Style and Titles shall hereafter require the assent as well of the Parliaments of all the Dominions as of the Parliament of the United Kingdom."

For three or four days, during which the newspapers on both sides of the Atlantic bristled with tantalizing surmises that Parliament would surrender to the King, or that a morganatic marriage would be allowed, there were busy exchanges between the Dominion Office in London and the Prime Ministers of Canada, Australia, South Africa, India, and New Zealand. The Dominion governments were asked—in scrupulously objective language, composed not by Baldwin but by Malcolm MacDonald, the Secretary of State for the Dominions—to say whether they favored a marriage in which Mrs. Simpson would become Queen; or a morganatic marriage in which she would not become Queen; or whether the King should abdicate. India was divided on religious grounds, the Muslims approving the King's proposal, the Hindus rejecting it. The Prime Minister of New Zealand was blithely agreeable to anything the King cared to do, though also to "anything the King's government did to restrain him." But Canada, Australia, and South Africa were adamant. They would not have Mrs. Simpson ("a woman twice divorced," as Queen Mary kept saying to herself and anyone else who questioned the feasibility of the marriage) as Queen, nor would they sanction a morganatic marriage.

To be quite sure that there was no party division at home, Baldwin consulted Attlee, the leader of the Labor opposition, who told him that "despite the sympathy felt for the King and the affection which his visits to the depressed areas had created, the [Labor]

Party—with the exception of a few of the intelligentsia who could be trusted to take the wrong view on any subject—were in agreement with the views I expressed." On his next visit to the King, Baldwin reported the overseas decisions and the confirming refusal of the Cabinet. Considering the King's limited acquaintance with English history, Baldwin charitably refrained from the elementary reminder that the King was bound by the constitutional rule of 1688: he was ultimately subject to the advice of his Ministers. And, like James II, he had to go.

The essential issue has never been more exactly put than by Harold Laski, in a dispatch printed in *The New York Times* three days before the abdication: "This issue is independent of the personality of the King. It is independent of the personality of the Prime Minister. It does not touch the wisdom or unwisdom of the marriage the King has proposed. It is not concerned with the pressure, whether of the churches or the aristocracy, that is hostile to this marriage. It is the principle that out of this issue no precedent must be created that makes the Royal authority once more a source of independent political power in the State."

After a hesitant day or two—while the public was distracted by the papers with flattering or questionable biographies of Mrs. Simpson, each paper playing one hunch or the other about the outcome—Parliament rallied swiftly to Baldwin's side when it appeared that there was a genuine threat of a King's Party, led by a Winston Churchill temporarily blind to the strength of the British Constitution. If that had come about, it might have heralded a national upheaval or even the end of the monarchy itself, for what enough sensible men saw was the profound anarchy inherent in a Parliament suddenly subdued by a royalist rump. (Said one mild, shrewd Member: "We should be looking round for a Cromwell again.") Reinforcing this fear, especially in the Labor Party, was a suspicion of the King's Nazi sympathies—a suspicion that did not have to wait to be confirmed by the publication, twenty years later, of the 1940 German documents. The luck of having George VI on the throne was applauded with much relief, within months of the abdication, when Edward committed the appalling gaffe of being entertained by Hitler and Goering on a mission limply described as a study of German "housing projects."

Edward clearly understood quite soon that he could not have Mrs. Simpson as his Queen without the consent of the Cabinet. But beyond that he had no grasp of the Constitution, only of protocol—a confusion that was to make his married life fretful for many years. It shocked him to discover that in the British system the monarch is the vessel of the monarchy and that once the vessel is changed the old monarch has at best a dubious status. The Duchess seems never to have learned this at all. Her autobiography, and the memoirs and reliable anecdotes about her, show a woman who labored and railed for years under the delusion that she was married to a King in exile, to whom influential Englishmen and women—including traveling members of the royal family—meanly refused to pay obeisance. The generosity of friends—the exclusive use of the Rothschilds' castle in Austria immediately after the abdication—appeared to Edward to be no more than his due. (He left, after a four months' stay, without thanking his hostess or tipping the servants.) And the generous concession of other governments seemed only to stress the churlishness of his own family. Thus, the French government leased him an imposing house in Paris at a nominal rent and allowed him the status of a tax-free citizen. The mere fact that to live in England would have cost him something in taxes, and more to maintain his royal style, was to him yet another example of his native land's vindictiveness. And once he had lost the power to practice noblesse oblige he became a stickler for noblesse. This "democratic" prince, who had been universally praised for his indifference to the regal formalities, is seen preparing for a dinner party in France by dispatching peremptory requests to London for all the decorations he had not bothered to wear at home. (Later, there was the little matter of a precious jewel which the royal family maintained belonged to the Crown. At some uncertain point, it was in the Duke's possession and so passed on to the Duchess.) When the new King (George VI) telephones him, the Duke leaves word that he will take the call only after dinner. Whereupon the mild George VI, who was always made out to be the stuttering, deferential brother, leaves a firm message that the Duke will take the call at the King's bidding.

The nagging fear of insult that this constitutional blindness entailed is not unlike what appears to have plagued the Nixons, besieged at San Clemente and testy with a similar sense of persecution. For what? For "mistakes of judgment" and lack of "decisiveness," not by any means for "high crimes and misdemeanors." In the same way, the sudden irrelevance of a lifetime's indoctrination as a King made the Duke in exile less and less willing to understand why he had had to go. Brooding away on the old wound, in Paris and Nassau and New York and Palm Beach, he saw it all ever more sharply as a calculated blow at his wife. Seeing his wistful face wizened in the later years, almost a David Levine caricature of jetset boredom, I could not help recalling the savage epitaph written by Westbrook Pegler the weekend the King quit the throne: "He will go from resort to resort getting more tanned and more tired." It seemed insufferably cruel at the time, for he had been only days before still the golden boy among the monarchs of the globe. But it was no crueler than the actuality—the thirty-five-year exile that lay ahead. The governorship of the Bahamas was no more than the gift of a sun lamp between the twilight grandeur of his eleven-month reign and the long night of his banishment to the transatlantic social tour: Cannes to Paris, to New York, to Palm Beach, back to the Waldorf, on to Paris, and back again. For all the sycophancy of his newfound court among the gossip-column aristocracy of retired manufacturers and brokers, real estate barons, bankers and cosmetics makers, he really had no place to go, and he knew it. Reduced to the company of such people, he took on their primitive, paranoid form of conservatism, which begins with alarm at any threat to their comfort, goes on to applause for "strong men" (Salazar, Franco) who can guarantee the protection of their luxury, and ends with an unsleeping fear of "radicals" and "Communists," of "them" against "us." The night he sailed away from England, Edward wrote to thank Baldwin for his kindness and "great understanding at this difficult time." Many years later, under the prodding of his wife and the prompting of his "ghost," Baldwin has turned into a "beetle" and a villain.

The most revealing picture of Edward as a permanently frustrated royal is not to be found in any official document or in the correspondence and reminiscences of retired officials who can usually be expected to geld a lively memory in the interests of good form or their own reputation. It comes alive in letters to a wife written from Austria and France by a faithful companion in exile, by Major Edward (Fruity) Metcalfe, whom the King himself once called his most loyal friend. He had served the Prince as aide-de-camp on his overseas tours. He served the Duke with and without pay during the first years of exile. When the Germans invaded France, the Duke decamped for Biarritz and abandoned Metcalfe in Paris without a word or a telephone message. From Metcalfe's jaunty letters one gets an unforgettable impression of the chronic irritability, the hypochondria, the fear for personal safety of a caged milord far from home.

On the third of September, 1939, the day Britain went to war with Germany, the Duke and his Duchess were in Cap d'Antibes, and the British government had agreed to send out an airplane to rescue them. Metcalfe wrote to his wife about his first and only blowup with the Duke:

We seem to be entirely cut off from the rest of the world, & we know "d——n all" of what is happening. . . . Certain people here are *quite extraordinary*. . . . On Friday it had all been settled for a plane to be sent out early Sat morning to bring us home, etc. . . . It all seemed plain sailing to me. I have become adviser in chief and the only person who is getting anything done here now & indeed they realize it. I, it was, who got all the servants off, 8 of them & 1 secretary. It took some doing, I can tell you as Cannes stn. was Hell on earth . . . Well anyhow they came in to me after about ½ hour & said "We are *not* going—the plane is coming for *you* & Miss Arnold tomorrow." I looked at them as if they really *were* mad—Then they started off—"I refuse to go *unless* we are invited to stay at Windsor Castle . . ." I just sat still, held my head & listened for about 20 minutes & then I started. I said *I'm* going to talk now. First of all I'll say that whatever I say is speaking as *your best* friend, I

speak only for your good & for W's, *understand
that* . . . You *only* think of yourselves. You don't
realise that there is at this moment a war going
on, that women and children are being bombed
& killed while you talk of your PRIDE . . . You
are just nuts. Do you really think for one instant
they would send a plane out for me & Miss
Arnold? It's too absurd even to discuss. I said a
lot more in the same strain. They never uttered.
After this I said now if this plane *is* sent out to
fetch you, which I doubt very much, then get into
it & be b——y grateful. I went to bed then. It was
3:15 a.m. . . . Then at 8 HRH came in *fully*
dressed to my room & said we've decided to go in
the plane. I said O.K. *if* it comes & now I'll have a
bath.

It is the only time one sees the Duke with all his
defenses down, shorn of authority or the pretense of it.
Lady Donaldson, again, was the one who exhumed
this pathetic memoir, and she makes the shrewd point
that throughout Edward's youth and early middle age
it was possible to see qualities of mind that were due
entirely to his being well briefed: "No one who has not
witnessed the difference in authority between someone
who has 'the papers' and the same person without them
can appreciate how much good briefing can mean."
Daily possession of "the papers" is, in fact, the main
and most deceptive perquisite of high office, and one
that conveys to the people of America, during more
presidencies than one cares to think about, an image of
authority and authoritativeness that is wholly absent
from the President-elect or even from ex-Presidents.
Edward comes out of it all as one of the least
enlightened of British monarchs—a charming, spoiled,
woefully ill-educated man, painfully simpleminded

and ferociously acquisitive. He is more to be pitied than abused in that the worlds of art, literature, music, politics, science, religion, philosophy—the whole life of the mind—were closed to him. At the end, says Lady Donaldson crisply, "he had three interests—golf, gardening, and money . . . and the greatest of the three was money."

There was also, it should be said, the most cherished interest of all: the lady who for half his life was mistress, wife, manager, companion, protector, disciplinarian, nurse, and sole beloved. That she was all these things to the end was the one salvation he rescued, and it must have been a consoling revenge against the gossips who circled like buzzards waiting through the years for the ultimate humiliation, which never came, of a broken marriage.

Falling back on a primitive theory of genetics, though it is one everybody believes in, I suggested earlier that he inherited his sensual, sybaritic side from his grandfather. But what he failed to inherit from anyone was that sense of decorum which, in the firm rhetoric of the Victorians—whether soldier, Empire builder, evangelist, or libertine—was called duty. Edward VII would have kept his throne through a dozen Mrs. Simpsons. Or perhaps it is better to say he would not have chosen even one of her kind. For the safety valves of all his liaisons were his own strong awareness of the duty code, the unthinkability of abdication, and the automatic acceptance of that code by the mistresses of the King's choice. In an historical sense, the fatal attraction of Mrs. Simpson may have been her transatlantic innocence, the intensity of emotion that an English or Continental mistress would have known from the beginning was too dangerous to indulge. Unlike Mrs. Keppel, unlike even Lady Warwick or Lily Langtry, Mrs. Simpson didn't know how far to go. From all familiar accounts, she learned to pay lip service to the discretionary code with admirable propriety. In the presence of the King's closest friends she addressed him, even in her chiding or skittish moments, as "Sir." She was at once so affectionate and so circumspect in public that she deceived even such a bilious onlooker as Chips Channon, who decided she was the best sort of mistress Edward could possibly have. (Maybe she was the best sort of wife, but as such she was a guarantee of the rupture.) The effect on Edward was to give him, for the only time in his life, both an adoring lover and a kindly, understanding mother. By the time he was King, he simply could not let her go.

And as he aged, he came to adopt the permanent, hurt attitude that he had been condemned to exile for nothing but his great love. He more and more saw himself as a martyr, and was assisted in his self-pity by his circle of American friends, harping on the downright view expressed, when he died, by Shana Alexander: "On this side of the water, the entire affair can only make sense as romance. As history, it was outrageous; mediaeval in its cruelty... beyond all human comprehension."

Well, as history, it could have been more than outrageous: it could have been bloody, if a revived King's Party had disrupted Parliament and plunged the country into a division between those who were for him and those against. During the worst time, the ten days that shook and toppled his throne, his private emotional turmoil hid from him the central fact, as inescapable as the pounding of his pulse, which for many years he refused to learn: that he had not been simply a lover defied but the mainspring of a constitutional crisis. I think he learned it later, with infinite reluctance, but was too proud to admit it. It may explain the persistence to the end of that wistful, baffled expression, as of a playful child that once stepped on a land mine.

All in all, few disasters in the history of the English Kings were more fortunate for the British people than the appearance in the Prince's social set of the divorcée from Baltimore. When the war came, and the social tone of the royal life had hardly recovered from popular suspicion, Britain found herself with a modest and dutiful King, a devoted Queen, and two bright children—a microcosm of middle-class dependability that saw the country through when the going was bad. The most damning epitaph you can compose about Edward—as a Prince, as a King, as a man—is one that all comfortable people should cower from deserving: he was at his best only when the going was good.

III

H. L.
MENCKEN

*The Public and
the Private Face*

THE YOUNG, I SUPPOSE, are always on their way
between one private admiration and another, and are
more cruel than most in despising the recent idol
whenever a new one appears. In the early 1930s, we
were caught in a profound shift in social values, and
because the collapse of the Western financial structure
was the most glaring catastrophe at hand, we naturally
tended to see this collapse as the failure of the capitalist
system. The more personally uncomfortable we found
ourselves in the Depression, the more the idols of the
first quarter of the century appeared to be traitors or
unfeeling lackeys of a decadent system. (The "System"
was then the sinister word, as the "Establishment" is
today.)

If I had been an American, I would undoubtedly
have worshiped H. L. Mencken in my college years and
gone around the campus carrying the latest issue of
The American Mercury as the Chinese, so we are told,

carry *The Thoughts of Chairman Mao*. I would
certainly have warmed to Mencken's crusade to crush
what he called "the marshmallow gentility" of the
prevailing American fiction and have run through the
doors he had thrown open to welcome the approaching
realists, Dreiser and Farrell and James M. Cain and
O'Neill and Sinclair Lewis. But almost as certainly I
would have recoiled with the rest of Mencken's college-
boy disciples when the Depression turned out to be his
Waterloo and Franklin Roosevelt his Wellington.

In Britain, our loyalties were not more tenuous than
those of any previous generation. But on both sides of
the Atlantic the 1929 crash gave us an urgent reason to
renounce, as pillars of the collapsing structure, the
idols we had worshiped. This, of course, is hideously
unfair. Our idols had no say in the time they were born.
And it was not to be expected that a man like Mencken,
who had described himself as "a larva of the
comfortable and complacent bourgeoisie," was going
to grow a new character in his fiftieth year. But when
the Depression came, the public fame of anyone who
had preceded it was suspect.

However, I was not an American. I was a young
Englishman at Cambridge between the years of 1927
and 1932. And Mencken was barely a name. We had
fatter fish to fry nearer home. We had other idols to
topple. But we toppled them on the same *post hoc,
propter hoc* principle: since the crash had come after
them, they and their values had probably contributed
to it. We were consequently morbidly sensitive to the
fame, and therefore the public face, of any old guru
who appeared to have let us down. In my lifetime, I
can't recall a time when revisionism was so swift and so
ruthless. Which is why I think it worth going into the
contrast between the ways it was practiced in Britain
and the United States, in those early years of the 1930s.

"PRIVATE FACES IN PUBLIC PLACES," wrote W. H. Auden, "are wiser and nicer than public faces in private places." It sounds at first like a tender tribute to the best sort of friend, the one unknown to fame, but is really a bad-tempered slap at fame itself, however well or ill deserved.

It was written at a time when the young Auden (like the old Auden), a shy and acutely self-conscious social animal, was much concerned with getting back at anyone who had the gift of confidence and social ease. And the most obvious targets, to sensitive young men at Oxford and Cambridge in the early 1930s, were upper- and upper-middle-class types who were seemingly untroubled by the Depression and the rise of the Nazis. That Auden himself—like Orwell and Day Lewis and the rest—was an upper-middle-class type only exacerbated his yearning to be at one with the working classes. This has been exhaustively remarked on, especially in Orwell's determination to be "down and out" and far from the detested milieu that bred him. But now that the political incentive to this attitude is dead and gone, what is striking about so much of the early Auden is the way he pounces on the social poise of landowners, county characters, men about town, rich fathers, all the public school types he had grown up with and among whom he had felt uncomfortable: "Interrogate their poises, in their rich houses"; "And proud bridge and indignant nostril,/Nothing to do but look noble."

Because the English, unlike the Americans, had an upper class that ran the whole political and social show, the arrogance of Auden's targets was presumed to be a capitalist attribute. It did not seem to occur to even the most sophisticated leftists of the time that arrogance might be a universal trait of those in authority. For the premise that the left labored under in those naive times was that if a capitalist society was run by proud and imperious types, the longed-for alternative of a Communist society must be run by humble and compassionate types. It took the ghastly revelations of trials and purges and the testaments of such refugees as Koestler to bring home the force of Brutus' point that the more absolute the authority, the more it tends to "disjoin remorse from power." Koestler had cowered before the "proud bridge and indignant nostril" a thousand miles from Britain, and, when he came to live there, decided "I would rather be ruled by Colonel Blimp than by a commissar."

IN REPUBLICAN AMERICA, there was a more widespread shift in values. In Britain there had been no proletarian literature worth the name, and there was to be almost none even through the 1930s, but in America, as early as the 1910s and early 1920s, there was a more vigorous social protest, less doctrinaire, more creative, in the work of such as Frank Norris, Jack London, Theodore Dreiser, Sherwood Anderson, James T. Farrell, and Sinclair Lewis. What the Depression did, in a country more classless, was to identify the Enemy as the plutocrats and the engineers of the Coolidge prosperity. So that the writers who had celebrated, even ironically, the prosperous frivolity of that time— Huneker, James Branch Cabell, most of all Scott Fitzgerald—were as suddenly discredited as the stock market. ("But, my God," cried Fitzgerald in a forlorn apologia, "it was my material, it was all I had to work with.")

It may seem odd that H. L. Mencken should have been a spectacular victim of the crash. More than anyone, he had skinned and blasted the values of the 1920s. But he had done it from the fortress of an older conservatism. Democracy he had jeered at as no more than an impulse of envy. And his distaste for the American upper crust had hardened into contempt for a plutocracy whose values at work were centered in the countinghouse and, at play, in the country club. He had little more use for the radicals than for the bankers. He longed for Jefferson's "aristocracy of talent and virtue." It was not an ideal likely to appeal to 13 million unemployed, or any longer to his recent disciples suddenly fired by the new, radical talents of Dos Passos, John Steinbeck, Clifford Odets, or Marc Blitzstein. In the awful silence of unemployment and poverty, Mencken's salvos against the prostrate bankers sounded gratuitous, against the genteelism of American writing irrelevant, against the chicanery of labor leaders tasteless.

When I came to know him, he was at the low ebb of his great reputation. But, as an Englishman, I was unfamiliar even with its high tide. Mencken's victims were unknown in England and his targets too exotic to mean much. An American friend of mine at Cambridge lent me a couple of his books; one of them, I remember, was his *In Defense of Women*. It seemed to me, as I have since discovered it seemed to most English readers, noisy and verbose, and his invective style was that of a blunderbuss cracking nuts. If I had a prejudice against him, it was not for his scorn of democracy or his early philippics against Franklin Roosevelt, who, in the campaign newsreels I saw in my first month in America, appeared to be a curiously posturing light tenor and surely no match for the somber baritone of Herbert Hoover. The reader will gather at once that these were the days of my political and literary innocence in the newfound land. In the course of settling into the Yale School of Drama, and whipping down to New York to see all the plays, I had come to meet several literary people. Thornton Wilder, John Mason Brown, John Cournos. Eliot I had known in England. It was well understood among all of them that Mencken was a spent rocket.

But then, in my second year, I moved to Harvard and registered for a course with the fascinating title of "The History of the English Language in America." It had to do with the written language only insofar as the recording, in crude phonetics, of Colonial town meetings offered clues to the way people spoke in the seventeenth century. It was, in fact, a course in pure linguistics and was conducted by one Professor Miles L. Hanley, a dogmatic and charmless man but as a detective of accents and their regional origins as impressive as Henry Higgins. The notion that American speech had a fascinating and separate history since the settling of the first colonies was evidently of minimum appeal in those days. There were only three of us in the class; the others were an English girl graduate of London University and a man from Georgia who was doing roadwork much of the time, researching his thesis on "New England words for the poached egg." (There were, it came out, two of them, and he pinpointed them with great accuracy on a map, showing white circles in all the places that called it a poached egg, and black circles where it was known as a dropped egg.)

It was natural for an Englishman in exile to be as interested in the different vocabularies of the two countries as in the history of their divergent speech habits. Since Francis Moore arrived in Georgia in 1735 and noticed that Americans "in barbarous English" called the bank of a river "a bluff," Englishmen have gone around with their little mental notebooks, excited, generation after generation, with what they take to be their personal discovery that the English of England and the English of America are different. I began to listen and record, and was encouraged to send these nuggets to Mencken by Professor Hanley, to whom Mencken was not the scourge of the Baptist South or the "booboisie" but the reigning expert on such things as Anglo-American equivalents and the vagaries, in his native land, of the phoneme. For a time, it appears, I was competing with a San Franciscan in supplying Mencken with the different names for cuts of meat, as of the English "sirloin" for American "porterhouse," the American "sirloin" for English "rump," the American "rib chops" for the English "best end."

One day I had a letter, postmarked Baltimore, which invited me to "come down here and share with me some of the gorgeous crabs that infest the protein factory of Chesapeake Bay." It was a highly individual invitation, and it was from Mencken, who had been so far a scrupulous correspondent, always sending very short but very prompt acknowledgments for my notes. I met him first in the back room of Schellhase's, and when I arrived, he was sitting there behind a stein of beer with A. D. Emart of the Baltimore *Sunpapers*. For some reason having to do with my preconception of a scourge calling sinners to repentance, I suppose I expected to see a florid giant, the local Balzac swiveling his huge bulk to bark at lackadaisical waiters.

What I saw was a small man so short in the thighs that when he stood up he seemed smaller than when he was sitting down. He had a plum pudding of a body and a square head stuck on it with no intervening neck. His brown hair was parted exactly in the middle, and the two cowlicks touched his eyebrows. He had very light blue eyes small enough to show the whites above the irises, which gave him the earnestness of a gas jet when he talked, an air of resigned incredulity when he listened, and a merry acceptance of the human race and all its foibles when he grinned. He was dressed like the owner of a country hardware store. (On ceremonial occasions, I saw later, he dressed like a plumber got up for church.) For all his seeming squatness, his movements were precise, and his hands in particular were small and sinewy.

Nothing much has come down in my memory from that first conversation except his genial manners, his air of extreme attentiveness to even the most trivial remarks, and a habit of signifying approval of any bearable opinion by chanting, "Yeah, yeah." He asked me to keep notes and suggestions coming and to be sure to stop in at his house whenever I was in Baltimore.

This was evidently the private face of a most public man, whom few people could stop to look at for the fire and smoke of his old reputation. I read a good deal of him subsequently and made a discovery which I now believe it is essential for any Briton to make who wishes to appreciate American writers, American humorists especially, on their own ground. Since the two languages are composed of a set of different tunes (what the phoneticians call intonation patterns), it follows that there is an American cadence or inflection—expressing pathos, sarcasm, skepticism, conviction, or whatever—which is often quite different from the English tunes that express these emotions. I first fell on to this simple but crucial truth when an English friend of mine returned a borrowed copy of a James Thurber book and John O'Hara's novel *Butterfield 8*, which was then being highly touted by the American critics. The friend found Thurber unfunny and O'Hara's dialogue unreadable. I asked him to read a passage of each, and it was obvious at once that he had no clue to the mock-tragic emotion that prompted Thurber's recital of some early disaster or other, and no feel for the emotions of an O'Hara conversation. Sometime later, I got a visiting Midwesterner to read the Thurber in a deadpan monotone, and my friend went from one chuckle to another. A resident American actor read aloud a couple of pages of the O'Hara, and my friend—who was an addict of American movies—heard the dialogue come alive as that of a man and woman trying to be casual in an emotional crisis.

Mencken, one might guess, would sound much the same in any accent, since his is a trenchant and formal style. But, after two years in America, I found—as you find with a foreign language—that developing acquaintance with the usual idioms throws into relief what is original. A good deal of what had seemed heavy or windy in Mencken began to appear as a parody of just such heaviness and pomp. I was soon able to forget the outlandish metaphors he had picked up from Nietzsche, the pretended omniscience of Macaulay, the often tedious shockability of Ambrose Bierce, and isolate—as a page reader isolates the central sense—those passages which, in Garry Wills's words, are "as natural as a sneeze, and just as important—a seizure of facile energy, emphatic, genial, harmless."

It was difficult in those days to maintain that Mencken was an urban Mark Twain, essentially a humorist covering up his disillusion with human society ("Democracy is the theory that the common people know what they want and deserve to get it good and hard") and his pity for the human condition ("Women always excel men in that sort of wisdom which comes from experience; to be a woman is in itself a terrible experience"). Every American you ran into in

the thirties came from some region or some sect or cult
that he had execrated and enraged. He had no sooner
delighted the country clubs by exposing the "idiocy" of
Socialism than he horrified them by condemning their
own "swinishness, timidity and cowardice." The New
England Brahmins had nodded lofty assent to both
these strictures, so he characterized *them* as the keepers
of "a slaughterhouse of ideas." Nobody knew where to
have him. He was against the American Legion as
much as it was against the Communists. He was
against the Communists as much as they were against
the Republicans. But what ought to be remembered
now is that when the Attorney General, with the
blessing of President Wilson, initiated a Red-hunt that
made the McCarthy era by contrast almost a judicial
inquiry, Mencken cried out with "an irresistible
impulse to rush out and crack a head—in other words,
to do something for common decency." And though he
aroused the wrath of the National Association for the
Advancement of Colored People by writing facetiously
about "coons" and "Aframericans," when the Negro
poet Countee Cullen was invited by the Baltimore City
Club to a party which he was then asked to leave,
Mencken wrote next day: "The City Club cads stood
by without a protest when Cullen was kicked out. He
did not come to eat with them but simply to talk with
them. That [the Emerson Hotel] has a rule forbidding
coons to talk in the hotel is outrageous. It would be
hard to match in Mississippi."

Clearly, I did not read these things while they were
happening, but coming on Mencken late and at a
distance, I was able to ignore the blaze of his legend
and recall the serene little man with the pot-blue eyes
and genial manners, and nothing cocky about him
except the angle of his cigar.

By the time I returned to America for keeps in 1937, I had acquired a no doubt selective view of the private Mencken, from whom I had continued to receive cheerful notes, acknowledgments of Anglo-Americanisms, and—after his wife had died—a short letter which, shorn of its attention to business, was stony with despair.

At his home on Hollins Street, a red-brick row house that reinforced the picture of a comfortably retired plumber, it was a frequent surprise to find visitors who, at first glance, were either old friends or nosy admirers dropped by to pay tribute. But as often as not they were his public enemies come to settle in spittle what they had failed to solve in print. Fuming clergymen appeared in Hollins Street determined to pronounce damnation on a man who had spent so much mean talent insisting that he was unholier than they. They were always disarmed to discover not only an affable and easy host but a knowing student of theology and, as the doctors and lawyers of his acquaintance discovered, a gifted amateur of medicine and jurisprudence, who was willing and qualified to discuss the burial rites of Egyptians, the theory of the grand jury, or the latest fashions in anesthesia. Many of his victims became good friends, and he never minded if they excoriated him in kind. If they were able. The rub here was that Mencken had the advantage of weapons. They usually chose indignation. He chose the English language, delivered quietly with his blood pressure under firm control. What astonished so many of these intending duelists was that, away from the public forum, he did not ask for approval of his ideas, only a decent discussion and then a truce accompanied by the sacrament, preferably, of a dry martini, which he once called "the only American invention as perfect as a sonnet." In all these later encounters with public adversaries, most of whom grew twitchy and then deferential when they got over the shock of so amiable, so changed a Mencken, he managed to imply the hope that they would both proceed according to the rules he had laid down in the middle of a fight with Upton Sinclair: "What I admire most in any man is a serene spirit, a steady freedom from moral indignation, an all-embracing tolerance... when he fights he fights in the manner of a gentleman fighting a duel, not in that of a longshoreman cleaning out a waterfront saloon. That is to say, he carefully guards his *amour-propre* by assuming that his opponent is as decent a man as he is, and just as honest—and perhaps, after all, right."

In 1937, I found Mencken eons away from his role as the old thunderer. Walter Lippmann had once said of him, "He denounces life and makes you want to live." Now, he merely denounced Roosevelt and made all but the most arrant Republicans want to yawn. He, who had mocked at all reformers as "jitney messiahs" and all politicians as "essentially third-rate men," had come out publicly for Alfred Landon for President and thereby offered Westbrook Pegler the theme for a lamentation on the sad metamorphosis of the old Mencken, "who was committed against everything that Mr. Landon represents from the bumbling pomposity and dumb arrogance of the Old Deal to honorary college degrees and lodge buttons.... Now we discover Mr. Mencken staggering down the street under the unwieldy weight of an enormous Landon banner, a sunflower in his lapel as big as a four-passenger omelette.... I expect to read soon that Mr. Mencken has joined the Shriners and the Elks and I hope to be present to cover the story when he joins the

Tennessee fundamentalists and is totally immersed in Goose Crick wearing a night shirt and blubbering 'Hallelujah, Brother' between plunges in the cleansing flood."

Friends of mine who were aware that I knew Mencken excused the acquaintanceship on the grounds that it was an irksome necessity of my interest in the American language, as you might forgive an apprentice cabinetmaker for having a Ku Kluxer as an instructor. But in fact, the acquaintance grew into friendship as I emerged from being a mere linguistic correspondent and became a fellow reporter. I had resigned from my job as the BBC's film critic and returned to America on an immigrant visa, a radical move that had been made financially possible by the fat check I had received from the National Broadcasting Company for covering the abdication of Edward VIII. After a precarious stretch as a free-lance journalist and broadcaster, I joined the London *Times* and the New York office of the BBC, and from then, through twenty-eight years with the *Manchester Guardian*, I remained primarily a foreign correspondent. Inevitably, the job forged new links with Mencken and we talked or corresponded less and less about linguistics and more and more about politics, about old and new Baltimore, and about the mores of the various regions of the country I was traveling in. It would be logical to assume that I was fatally affected by Mencken's derision of the New Deal and his hatred of Roosevelt. But while we might argue about the plausibility of this fact or that rumor, he never questioned my right to a contrary opinion. In the interests of good fellowship we agreed not to bring up the name of the loathsome Roosevelt, whom he jocosely refused to call the President, tossing in instead snorting references to

"Franklin the First" or "Roosevelt the Second," or "Our Lord and Master," more often simply "The Crooner."

The odd thing about my friendship with him was that I amalgamated in one person a good many human types he disliked. He distrusted Englishmen, and abominated broadcasting, which had become my trade; he said that broadcasters suffered from "perfumed tonsils." He despised Methodists, and although I was relapsed, I had been brought up as one. Luckily, I had not then taken up golf, which I came to regard as a holy exercise but about which he had written: "I well recall my horror when I heard, for the first time, of a journalist who had laid in a pair of what were then called bicycle pants and taken to golf: it was as if I had encountered a studhorse with his hair done up in frizzes. . . . If I had my way, any man guilty of golf would be ineligible for any office of trust under these United States."

However, human chemistry, as it can, prevailed over a lifelong prejudice, and unlike most giants of idiosyncrasy, he never assumed that his truth, however insistently he proclaimed it, was *the* truth. He well understood that a foreign correspondent has to attract readers to something they are not naturally interested in and so must vary his output between entertainment and reportage. But while Mencken could pass out a compliment for a piece that was frankly satirical or opinionated, he reserved his serious praise for unvarnished pieces of reporting that tried to strike a balance between the known and probable facts, no matter whose side they came down on. He taught me, what I confirmed many times on the road, that there is no such thing as ideological truth, and that to the extent that a reporter is a liberal reporter or a Communist reporter or a Republican reporter, he is no reporter at all. This is not the same as saying that a good reporter is nothing if not "objective," and that outside the blank reportage of the news agencies every touch of anger, humor, or irony amounts to special pleading. There are times when the most seemingly fair-minded compilation of "facts" is dedicated, unwittingly or not, to giving equal weight to two sides of an argument and leaving the reporter at the end firmly on the fence. There are other, and rarer, times when what looks like a frankly partisan commentary is actually a careful archaeological dig which produces a set of surprising facts that will bear only one interpretation. By that test, some of the best reporting is done by columnists who are generally thought to be flying under one ideological flag or another. James Cameron's account of the means by which the British Colonial Office exploited and bankrupted the wretched Banabans of Ocean Island is factual reporting which leaves no other conclusion than that it was a "rapacious and squalid swindle." And William Safire's recounting of the number of Carter Cabinet and sub-Cabinet appointees who were directors of IBM amply supported the implication that if they had been nominated by a Republican President, the Democrats in the Senate would have raised an unholy row.

Old Mencken readers who remember him as the archetype of the city atheist bawling from his private pulpit may be forgiven for doubting that he was ever devoted to scientific method—that is, to discovering generalizations that cover all the known facts. But in the competing din of the cheers and boos for his invective style what has been forgotten—unfortunately never noticed by his more abject admirers—is that in the years of his active legwork, he produced some of the most remarkable reporting of his or any other day. His 1917 account, for instance, of the uprising in Cuba of the liberal José Miguel Gómez against the conservative President Menocal is a fantasia as comical and improbable as anything in Mark Twain. But for all its embroidery it is astonishingly close to the sequence of the facts as set down by the *Encyclopaedia Britannica*, fourteenth edition. And his report of exactly how Franklin Roosevelt came to be nominated in 1932, though it was written through the sweaty dawn of the Chicago convention, remains after forty-five years the most accurate and perceptive account of the forces at work behind the facade of the banners and the bunting.

I saw less of him during the Second War, mainly I now think because his stubborn refusal to see it as anything but a collision of powers equally fraudulent and hypocritical was something I—as a British correspondent in the United States—would have found too uncomfortable to contend with. But even then, he was always on hand to defend the rights of a reporter, whichever side he might privately be on. He encouraged me, early in 1943 I believe, to file for my London paper a protest against the severe censorship, at the American end, of dispatches that reported incompetence and worse on the industrial home front. And he was an unhesitating ally in a small private feud I had with the government when it bowed to a wave of suspicion about all foreign-born Americans and required me to sign up under an Aliens Registration Act. I was in the peculiar position of being the only working British correspondent who was also an American citizen. The other foreign correspondents, properly or reluctantly, filed their forms. But I saw no reason why, as an American, I should be suddenly demoted to the status of a resident alien, one, moreover, who—according to the Office of War Information official who was in touch with me—would be officially lumped as an acknowledged purveyor of British propaganda along with the employees of the British Information Services. I telephoned Mencken, and he raised his piping tenor to a bellow: "Who are the people who want you to do this?" I told him that I was being harassed by the OWI. "The OWI?" he shouted. "A gang o' draft dodgers. Tell 'em you won't sign, and tell 'em to go to hell." I conducted the final interview in considerably milder terms, but I was craven enough to mention that my friend Mr. Mencken had told me mine was a special case and that to declare myself a British propagandist would be an affront to both my trade as a reporter and my status as an American citizen. The listening official, a heavy-lidded New York socialite, well over age for military service, smiled ruefully at the name of Mencken, shook his head, and said, "Well, I'm afraid his argument is unanswerable." That was the end of that.

Throughout the war, Mencken himself did no reporting and, as a workaday journalist relegated to the sidelines, was a restless and unhappy man. He was at all times devoted to his beloved *Sunpapers*, but during those seven years, he had been having a polite but sullen feud with the publishers, most distressingly with his old friend Paul Patterson. The core of it is probably encrusted by now with innumerable small indignities and protective recriminations. But the original sore truth was that Mencken had hoped to keep up through the war years his incorrigible attacks on democracy and to go on writing about Hitler as a harmless jackass with a new broom, a late entry for Mencken's private menagerie of demagogues: William Jennings Bryan, Gerald K. Smith, "The Rev." Woodrow Wilson, and the rest. But the shiploads of refugee Jews who came into America soured the joke as early as 1938, if not before. And the attested rumors about Belsen and Buchenwald turned it rancid.

I have to say that I don't remember Mencken ever admitting that the gas chambers and the concentration camps existed. That he half believed they did was obvious from the uneasiness with which he brushed aside any mention of Nazi brutality and in a weary grumble equated such rumors with the First World War legend that the Germans had made soap out of the bodies of Belgian and French civilians. While he deplored the persecution of the Jews, his reluctance to face the glaring horror of the murdered Jews was pathetic. To admit it was so would have torn up the roots of his deep prejudice that the Germans were a sound and scholarly people, not less humane than other nations, and that any reasonable case that could be made out for them had been, as in the First War, stifled by the Anglomaniacs in the government and the universities. So, as he had done after he was a reporter behind the German lines the first time round (he was childishly proud of the fact that the Kaiser had declared himself a Mencken fan), he dug his heels into his Germanic background and exaggerated both its aristocratic disdain and its earthly common sense.

By 1941 at the latest, Mencken's playful treatment of the war was a daily trial to Paul Patterson. And when the paper came out on the interventionist side, Mencken affected to be a hireling of "world savers." To everyone's relief, he quit his column. At his own insistence, he went on half pay as something vaguely called a "news consultant," retiring to edit his files on the American language and to salvage his father's old household bills for a book about his boyhood. I can see him in that time moving rather more often than usual between his upstairs study, with its crested German shields defiantly hung on the walls, and the bathroom. He was a compulsive hand washer and rarely got through a piece without retreating to the washbasin five or six times. He was a day-long chewer of unlit cigars. And when he wasn't trotting off to Johns Hopkins Hospital to have himself "tapped and filtered," he would make a list on his worst days of all the rheums, tics, and eruptions he was suffering from at the moment. His ribald dissenting opinions were now available only to a shrinking circle of his friends in the back room at Schellhase's.

And yet this voluntary exile forced him into what turned out to be his most productive period, and the one in which he did what I should guess will come to be seen as the best and most memorable of his writing: the three volumes of his autobiography, *Happy Days, Newspaper Days,* and *Heathen Days.* His industry during this lonely time was prodigious. He finished for publication his personal anthology of his writings, *A Mencken Chrestomathy*, completed a twenty-five-year project, his *New Dictionary of Quotations*, and put out two massive *Supplements* to his parent volume, *The American Language.* The second *Supplement* came out in the spring of 1948, and he was on the cover of the newsmagazines, looking very pink and spry, one elbow up against the ghastly Victorian glass bells that his wife had treasured. But he was brooding even more than usual on the frailty of the human body in general and his own aches and twinges in particular. In the preface to *Supplement Two*, he wrote that he did not expect to attempt a third supplement since "at my age a man encounters frequent reminders, some of them disconcerting, that his body is no more than a highly unstable congeries of the compounds of carbon." I wrote a review of this for my paper and wound up a tribute to him with the sentence: "Who would have thought the old man had so much carbon in him?" The day after he received the clipping I had a note from him in which he said that he was "still blushing" and speculating where we should next celebrate "my declining faculties with a globe of malt." I wrote back to wonder if he would be tackling the presidential nominating conventions, a suggestion he repulsed with such horror that he was plainly very taken with the idea.

It seems, however, that by then Patterson and his son Maclean had been after him for months. The wartime feuds were fading, and they were very willing to forgive and forget. They gingerly fed him the bait of the conventions. Ten years earlier, nothing would have been more proudly taken for granted. Mencken had "begun to sniff at politicians so long ago as 1902" and had covered his first convention at St. Louis with the Democrats in 1904. For the next thirty-six years, a convention was to him the arrival of the circus to a country lad. Once every four years he went to work on them with his self-confessed "impartiality," which is to say the Hippocratical zeal of a surgeon who picks the same scalpel to excise the appendix of a Boy Scout or a dope peddler.

But Mencken had been deeply wounded by the rift, and yet, as a professional anesthetist of all public forms of sentiment, he was too proud to say so. He knew well enough that the *Sunpapers* had stretched to the limit their tolerance of his unpalatable jokes about Hitler, his mockery after Dunkirk of "those great moral engines, the British," his mischievous relish of such overtures as Churchill had to make to Rumania so as "to enlist King Carol in the holy war for religion and morality." He was probably also guiltily aware that few papers in any country, and none in America, would have conceded him for so long his dogmatic principle that a man should be allowed to say and publish whatever he thought, even in wartime. His frustration at Patterson's new approach was complicated by the fact that he was at all times secretly sentimental about his friendships and allegiances, and he had been the chief glory of the *Sunpapers* for a quarter of a century at least. Now that they raised a furtive white flag, he was touched. He bore his wound in silence, but he yearned for the salve they held out to him. And at last he took it.

He wrote to me again with the glee of a boy who has been given his first set of tickets to a World Series. He looked forward to "a banner year, one in which there will be not two but three circuses." (After the Republicans and the Democrats, there was to be the convention of the new Progressive Party, led by Henry A. Wallace, who had had a troublesome time staying with the Democrats. He had been Secretary of Agriculture and Vice President under Roosevelt, who dropped him without forewarning in favor of Harry S. Truman for the fourth term. He had been Secretary of Commerce under Truman and was fired by him for insubordinate criticism of the administration's stiffening policy toward the Soviet Union. Wallace accordingly quit the party, turned sharp left, and formed the Progressive Party.)

In the summer of 1948, Mencken was within two years of his biblical allotment. As a lifelong hypochondriac, he was more fearful of its coming, as a kind of D-day, than most men of sixty-eight, and he felt the east wind in his bones. He pasted down his cowlicks, now gone white and wispy, with more determination than usual, put on a new seersucker suit, stuffed it with enough cigars for a siege, picked up his portable old Corona, and headed for Philadelphia. There he sat, as anonymous as any other old reporter, wedged in along the wooden press benches under the bristling glare of the high arc lights, pecking out incomparably saucy

sentences on his typewriter with that deliberate manual
incompetence which is still one of the professional
reporter's occupational vanities. Mencken carried it to
the extreme of parody, hitting the keys only with his
tiny forefingers and spacing with his right elbow, a
routine that made him look like a bear cub imitating a
drum majorette. He would glare in a steady trance at
the keyboard while the loudspeakers rattled with the
sobs and bawlings of the party chieftains, and would
then slap out a woeful salute to "the traditional
weather of a national convention...a rising tem-
perature, very high humidity, and lazy puffs of
gummy wind from the mangrove swamps surrounding
the city."

The shift from the turkish bath of the convention
hall and the oven of the city to an air-conditioned
bedroom in the *Sunpapers*'s suite at the Ritz was too
much for him. He caught a bad cold, squaked and
stormed about the lethal novelty of air conditioning,
announced that he was no use to man or beast when his
sinuses were inflamed, and retired from the
Republicans and went snuffling home to Baltimore.
But he was back for the Democrats, still muttering
about air conditioning as probably an invention
("subsidized with federal funds") of Roosevelt the
Second. But he was wedged in the trenches again in
time to goggle at the fetching appearance of Mrs.
Dorothy Vredenberg, secretary of the Democratic
National Committee. At both the Democrats' and the
Progressives' conventions, I had the luck, contrived by
Patterson, to draw the working press seat next to
Mencken, so I had the experience of watching the old
man at work night and day. He typed out his stuff in
triple space, on a ribbon that might well have been
installed at the 1904 convention. But however faint and
gray was the typescript, the sharp prose was no one's

but his. He looked up at Mrs. Vredenberg and looked down to tap out that she was "uniquely slim and smartly clad." He looked at her again, mumbled, "This is unprecedented," and added that she had triumphantly outraged the tradition that "lady politicians shall resemble British tramp steamers dressed up for the King's birthday." He was in rare form, and he knew it: determined to show that he was a working newspaperman to the end.

None of us, including Mencken, knew how near the end was. For this turned out to be his last reporting stint, and very nearly his last piece of writing. August and September were always a weeping ordeal for him, since he regularly collapsed under the seasonal hay fever. He emerged dry-eyed and in his right mind by November, but on the twenty-third of that month he suffered a cerebral thrombosis, which left him with a semantic aphasia. His sight was unimpaired, but he could no longer make what he saw coincide with what it meant. All writing, printing, public signs were well-focused gibberish. He never picked up a pen or a book, or stared at a typewriter, after that. So the Wallace convention was his last fling, the last stretch of what he would never know again as happy days.

Before the last convention—all three were held in Philadelphia—he had written to assure me that "the Wallace show will be the best of all." He cautioned me not to pass up the meeting of the platform committee, which was to get under way the evening before the convention was formally called. I met him there, in a hotel ballroom, and we sat through the long hours while the committee patiently canvassed an earnest horde of reformers and malcontents from most of the states and all, it seemed, of the territories and inland possessions.

In the chair was Rexford Guy Tugwell, a sincere

New Deal renegade (I suggested). "A scoundrel of the first chop," said Mencken, and put down a note to that effect. This was my sixth convention, but like everybody under sixty or so, I was a novitiate at Progressive performances, and I was fascinated by the range of zealots who had come into Philadelphia consumed with some private obsession: nationalization of the banks, the railroads, and the merchant marine was a familiar parrot cry. So was the immediate repudiation of the Marshall Plan, repeal of the Taft-Hartley Act, the abolition of state and city taxes, not to mention "the end of the colonial system in all its forms." But I was shaken by the tremors of passion given off by delegates who—just when the Russians were threatening a European war over Berlin—were exclusively dedicated to liberating Puerto Rico, or drafting a safety code for longshoremen, demanding a Cabinet post for the fine arts or federal funds for dentistry. "Wait awhile," Mencken whispered, "any minute now you're going to get Oswald Garrison Villard and salvation through the thirty-hour day."

Toward one in the morning, the newsmen began to decamp, but Mencken stayed to the end, plugging his poker face with the inevitable cigar and remarking that while the Progressives had produced "a surprisingly good crop, they have nothing so bizarre" as the eccentrics he swore he had seen at the Bull Moose Convention of 1912. On the way out we ran into a liberal journalist who introduced himself to apologize for a boorish review of *Supplement Two* done by a friend of his in the *New Masses*. Mencken turned his pot-blue eyes on the man. "Tell me something," he said, "are you a liberal?" The man said that was right. "Well, now," said Mencken, "I thought that was a fine review. The man wrote what he thought, and I must say it was a swell piece of writing." The man was much

118

relieved. "The trouble with you liberals," Mencken called after him, "is you get uneasy when people don't agree with you."

It was very late, and I assumed that Mencken, after so much recent moaning about his approach to the grave, would beg off on account of his sinuses and go to bed. But again he appeared to want to show that he was as casually professional as any other reporter, who on such assignments behaves like an oblivious infantryman, snatching sleep and food only when the firing lets up or the liquor has all gone. He knew a place where we could get German beer, and we downed a barrel of it in the conviction that "hoisting schooners of malt" was the best possible preparation for a two-day bout of Henry Wallace as a presidential candidate.

When we got back to the party's hotel headquarters, the faithful were still up, milling around the entrance and embracing on the steps. To a veteran of the two regular parties, they were an odd lot. It was a slow-paced crowd by the usual standards and in the full bloom of bohemian youth. Many of the men had their collars folded back over their lapels, at that time a sign of an emancipated clerk at Atlantic City or a fledgling Los Angeleno. The women divided sharply between down-to-earth, no-nonsense types with sandals and off-the-shoulder Mexican blouses, and thin brunettes wearing earrings as long as icicles meant to convey the piercing, onstage elegances of Greenwich Village *femmes fatales*. Wandering like scoutmasters through these political innocents were older, blue-chinned men who might have been union secretaries, economics professors up against "the System," or schoolmasters with a new purpose in life. There was a generous sprinkling of Negroes, most of them slender and studious.

Outside the hotel, on trucks got up as miniature

carrousels, small groups of young people danced and plucked expertly at guitars, and sang lampoons of old hymns, folk tunes with new words, and the Wallace campaign songs. As we arrived, a Youth for Wallace brigade was proclaiming the wide, Whitmanesque representation of the new party, a merry crew (nowhere in evidence) of

> Lumberjacks and Teamsters,
> And sailors from the sea;
> And there's farming boys from Texas
> And the hills of Tennessee;
> There's miners from Kentucky
> And there's fishermen from Maine,
> All a-ridin' with us
> On this Wallace-Taylor train.

(Glen Taylor, Wallace's running mate, had been described by Mencken as "a third-rate mountebank from the great open spaces.... Soak a radio clown for ten days and nights in the rectified juices of all the cow-state Messiahs ever heard of and you have him to the life." This was not the sort of tribute that endeared Mencken to the Progressives.)

Mencken stood on the steps of the hotel, allowing that the older parties could learn a lot about singing from the Wallaceites, and groaning only slightly over the determined illiteracy of their syntax. Some sad-faced older women sifted in and out to recruit the idlers. To all of them Mencken gave little ducking bows, bulging his eyes in sly admiration of the passably pretty females and letting them catch a hoarse echo of various compliments: "What grace, what style! ... I never saw such ravishing creatures." Bowing his way out of the crowd, and hailing the men as "Comrade," he went across the street and into the Ritz. Nobody had the slightest idea who he was.

Next afternoon, the official proceedings got off to a furious start in a press conference with Wallace. He was a strange type to have gone into politics: a mystic, a lifelong farmer with a researcher's devotion to breeding hybrid strains, a man who had picked up an evangelical concern for humanity but had little affection for human beings. He had a strong strain of Maugham's Mr. Davidson in him, an irritableness with human frailty and a hectoring insistence on words like "peace," "justice," the "common man" as if they were inventions of his on which nobody cared to take up the patent.

He was rigid from the start and made the elementary blunder of starting with a scolding little sermon against the press itself. He knew, he said, he knew very well that "you are all desperately hoping" he would repudiate the Communists. Well, "I will not repudiate any support that comes to us in the cause of peace." (One likely explanation of his bristling behavior was that he was even then feeling the pull, and resenting it, of the small tenacious crew of Communists, and near-Communists, who had already taken over the party and who, the next morning, were to slam through a sheepish convention in forty minutes a "constitution" for the new party so absurdly patterned after all Communist constitutions that two hardy New England farmers were flabbergasted at the smothering of all dissent or debate and admirably stalked out of the hall to thunderous boos.) It was not, however, the Communists that flushed Wallace's face that afternoon, though his guilt about their commanding power was such that he was visibly sprouting chips on his shoulders. He feared, and rightly, that he was going to

121

be joshed, at best, for the so-called Guru letters, a rambling mystical correspondence with a Russian named Roerich which Westbrook Pegler had somehow procured and printed in his newspaper column above the signature of Henry Wallace.

Sure enough, someone rose at once and asked him to say if he was indeed the author. He snapped in reply, "I never discuss Westbrook Pegler." A girl from a friendly radical sheet asked the same question. He intoned the same answer. Suddenly the room gasped as a big man with sandy-white hair got up. It was Pegler himself, glowering back at Wallace like a bull just released into the ring.

"Did you or did you not write the Guru letters?"

Wallace was beyond flushing by now. He tried to look casual. "I will never," he chanted, "engage in any discussion with Westbrook Pegler."

Three others put the same question. To each of them, Wallace recited in an obdurate singsong that he would "never engage in any discussions with stooges of Westbrook Pegler."

The reporters were beginning to sigh or giggle or tap their feet. Then Mencken was seen by the people near him to be on his feet. To everybody else he looked, as he always did in a public gathering, to be risen to his knees, and young reporters, who had heard about the Mencken legend but knew nothing more about him, craned from the back rows or stood on chairs to see him. In a voice so gentle that it belied that legend and caused one or two people to ask him to speak up, he said, "Would you consider *me* a Pegler stooge?" The laugh started before Wallace could hush the applause. His face relaxed into something we didn't think him capable of: a grin. "No, Mr. Mencken," he said, "I would never consider you anybody's stooge."

"Well, then," said Mencken, infinitely solicitous,

"it's a simple question. We've all written love letters in our youth that would bring a blush later on. There's no shame in it. This is a question that all of us here would like to have answered, so we can move on to weightier things."

Wallace swallowed and in a steadier voice said he would "handle that in my own time." So far as I know, he never did and so—as Sterne once wrote—he "put upon the reader the odium of the obvious interpretation."

That night the party christened itself the Progressive Party in the convention hall and sat with unusual intentness through the keynote speech, which was delivered by an Iowa lawyer, a handsome and substantial Negro with a soaring baritone voice. Mencken described him as easily the best of all the orators that had appeared in Philadelphia that summer, but he slipped into his dispatch the typical note that the man had "the complexion of a good ten-cent cigar." Next morning, a well-plotted uproar developed when the convention met to chant "aye" to the draft constitution. Silence was prayed for a resolution pronouncing that "whereas H. L. Mencken is guilty of Hitlerite references to the people of this convention," that he "Red-baits, Jew-baits, and Negro-baits" and in other noxious ways had indulged in "un-American slander of the people of this convention . . . therefore be it resolved by the delegates here assembled, That this convention severely censures H. L. Mencken and his contemptible rantings which pass for newspaper reporting."

Mencken goggled with unaccustomed pride. It was the first time in all his reporting years that a national convention had officially deigned to regret his existence, although the Arkansas state legislature had once petitioned for his deportation. He took a small bow to acknowledge the passing tribute of a boo, but the resolution got no further. The chairman threw it out as a dangerous precedent inviting an endless litany of curses against other blasphemers, of whom there were plenty.

(This is as good a place as any to lay the myth of Mencken's "Jew-baiting," which was first propagated by a disappointed editor Mencken once fired. Jews are naturally going to be suspicious of any man who identifies another man in print as a Jew, unless in a religious context. In view of a couple of thousand years of persecution, this is an understandable reflex, but it is still hypersensitive. And to such people, to point out that Mencken had throughout his life close friendships with Jews will only invite the sneer that "sure, some of his best friends were Jews." In fact, most of his best friends were Jews, whom—once in an hierarchical grouping of nations and races—he placed "as superior to the Americans, as the Germans are superior to the Jews." He would not have written that during the Second War. For all his facetious pretense that the Nazi regime "had its points compared with the New Deal," he despised the Nazis' persecution of the Jews as he condemned their suppression of all civil liberties. It was Mencken who, at a time when liberals deemed it politic to keep their mouths shut during the Communist hunt of the twenties, came out fighting to stop the deportation of Emma Goldman. If, in the last quarter of our century, his flip characterizations of particular people by their nationality or region seem tasteless, in the first quarter of the century his assumption that everybody he dealt with—of whatever race or persuasion—was to be treated as an equal was rare. When he wrote that Freud "as a Jew...will probably fall victim to some obscure race war in Vienna," he was not making an anti-Semitic remark but an all too accurate prophecy. It is quite untrue to say, as a recent reviewer of his published letters has written, that "he runs over with simple dislike for Jews, blacks, Poles, teetotalers, and dogs." It *is* true that he disliked puritans, teetotalers, Communists, Englishmen, Methodists, and politicians on principle. But if one presented himself who was otherwise a rational and agreeable man, he spontaneously filed and forgot his prejudice. As for the blacks, he always lamented the wretched conditions in which most of them lived and saved his contempt for the Southern— or Northern—whites who thought of themselves as the black man's superiors.)

The night of the anti-Mencken resolution, we sat down to a slab of beef and some beer, and Mencken complained about "the growing sensitiveness of politicians. Nobody denounced me as a white-baiter," he said, "when I wrote that Herbert Hoover had a complexion like unrisen dough." He took a swig and broke down into his schoolboy-crafty grin, and we took off for the final rally in Shibe Park. On the way out there, he was in a frisky mood, grumbling with great gusto over the faceless uniformity of American cities, of their slummy petticoats especially, and recalling with a contrasting tenderness San Francisco and the Democratic Convention of 1920.

When the rally was over and the Progressive Party was a fact, if only for the year of its inception, there were rolling black clouds overhead. The wind shifted, the atrocious heat gave out, and there was a miraculous chill in the air which sent us nipping back to the Ritz. Paul Patterson had arranged a farewell party in his suite for the *Sunpapers* team; and since the *Manchester Guardian* had had a long and friendly connection with the *Sunpapers*, and I had been working throughout the convention out of their quarters, I was the only invited guest. A table was laid out with sandwiches, beer, and whiskey. At the start, visitors would drop in, but the gathering was as cliquish as the Mafia, and they would soon excuse themselves after a self-conscious nibble at the viands reserved for the family. The last interloper was Dorothy Thompson, who then was a lady journalist of declining fame and rising girth. She was drawn to the food like a castaway and kept wolfing it helplessly and declaring between gulps that her doctor had warned her against letting her figure go to rack and ruin.

Mencken twirled his cigar in his lips and relieved the general embarrassment by professing to be shocked at such an obviously inept diagnosis. "Never trust the medicos and the butchers, Dorothy," he cried, and after a pause and a puff, "Why, Dorothy, you were never lovelier, you were never in better heft." He went on this way, and it was a relief to all of us to see Miss Thompson wriggle her great frame in simple delight. She was the only woman present, and after a while she too sensed our trade-union impatience with her and left. She was no sooner heard plodding down the corridor than Mencken looked at the froth on his stein and said sadly, "My God, she's an elephant, isn't she?"

Through what was left of the night, Mencken sat on a central sofa between Price Day and me. From here he could survey the reigning Patterson and his buffet table on the left, and the ring of reporters lounging and squatting all the way over to the windows. (There is implicit in this sentence a deception I have touched on before that is common to all biographical mementos. This is a piece about Mencken, and therefore he is bound to be the hero of it, or at least the central figure. He was not so treated at the time. He never condescended to anyone, certainly not to professional newspapermen.) He sat simply as an old reporter among equals. And for an hour or more nothing happened to make him the comic hero of an occasion that grew to be more memorable and more precious only three months later, when his sudden stroke guaranteed that this was to be his last bit of horseplay on this earth.

Shortly after one in the morning, our small talk and anecdotage were interrupted by a commotion reaching us from the street. We heard a stamping and a singing. Someone threw open a window. Evidently, a detachment of Wallace's soldiers was making a stand outside the Ritz, as handy a symbol as any of the "finance capitalism" that was Wallace's favorite hobgoblin. Paul Patterson had the waggish idea that we should invite them up, and Mencken seconded it briskly, "because at the very least we could sing, since they certainly have the catchiest numbers." Yardley, the *Sunpapers*'s cartoonist, was sent out after them, and shortly afterward the stamping and cheering died away. Yardley came back with the word that they had scattered and fled, and we were about to forget them when there was a scuffle somewhere nearby, right in the hotel. It grew denser and came on louder in our direction till it passed, like Marley's ghost, right through our door. "It" was five or six of the Minnesota Youth for Wallace battalion, the leader being a giant of a black-haired Swede. He stood scowling at us. He was bearing a banner with the help of a jumpy little man and a shapeless, dropsical blonde. Mencken gaped at them in genuine alarm. But it was not alarm over their belligerence. His eye had fallen on the female archetype of the young radical. "My God," he whispered to Day and me, "just look at that woman. Makes you want to burn every bed in the world." Day nearly fell off the sofa, and the rebels took it as a sign that we were jeering at them, which, come to think of it, we were.

127

"So who are you all, anyway?" the leader challenged.

It was a brash note to begin on, but Patterson caught it tolerantly and replied quietly, "We are the press, ladies and gentlemen—the capitalist press."

Mencken looked innocently over the ash of his stogie and added mildly, "Except Mr. Cooke here, of the—er—London *Daily Worker*."

At one bound, the jumpy little man shot out from underneath the banner. He seized my hand and shouted in delight. "No kidding? D'you know Rhoda—in London?" To this day I think tenderly of Rhoda, whoever she was, and the bond that linked her first with Minnesota and then with our besieged group. The greeting produced even more confusion among the Minnesotans, and when another reporter made it plain through the ensuing guffaws that the *Guardian* was my paper, the jumpy guy wilted and the black Swede fumed again. Patterson invited them to eat, an unnecessary kindness, since two of them, including the blonde, had been doing some fast stoking under the flapping tent of the Wallace banner.

Mencken at last persuaded them to "furl the flag" and settle to a singsong. He made a naive, artful pretense of having forgotten the "swell lyrics" of their best songs. They leaped to the cue like the converts by the Tennessee brooks whom Mencken had long ago observed. And we all gave voice and began:

> *Lumberjacks and Teamsters,*
> *And sailors from the sea;*
> *And there's farming boys from Texas...*

When they saw how well some of the reporters knew their songs, they lost or at least modified their suspicion of us. Mencken sighed occasionally over the more gruesome lines ("Oh, Henry Wallace is a friendly man" was one, I recall, that pained him immoderately). When we had exhausted the whole Wallace hymnal, Mencken stood up and buttoned his tight coat. One of the team thought he was coming at them. (I doubt that any of them knew he was the "Un-American Mencken" of the lost resolution. With his red homely face, his white hair slit down the middle, his stocky legs, he might well have been the proprietor of a delicatessen store that had catered the food.) He raised his very small hand and got attention. He proposed that since we had so lavishly celebrated "our beloved Fuehrer" (the Minnesotans looked blank and must have thought of Hitler, if of anybody), "it is only right that we now salute the Republic he hopes to preside over."

This sort of talk, which was as natural to Mencken as breathing—rather more so in the ragweed season— baffled them completely until he said, "Now, let's try our national anthem." He held his finger up and tilted his head and piped out several wobbling notes. He picked something about as impractical as F Major and led off with a fluting tenor. He let them take it away after a few bars and muttered to me: "Just wait till they hit the middle; it will really throw them." The citizens' chorus lurched up to the necessary and impossible E, squawked in alarm, and broke down. They looked to Mencken for help, but he had stuck his cigar between his lips and was grinning through his eyes.

The leader took this badly and growled something about the national anthem's being nothing to make fun of. Mencken agreed with a marvelously affected humility but admitted that "as a practical matter we have paid our respects to our great anthem, which is unsingable anyway."

More beer was rushed to the visitors, and just as we sat down, Mencken rose again. He put his cigar

between his thumb and forefinger and held it up like
the stump of a baton. He had one more favor to ask of
the visitors. We had, he thought they ought to know,
just afflicted on "an alien and a special guest the
caterwaulings of the official hymn of our Republic."
He thought it only "seemly" that they should all now
pay respects "to His Majesty King George the Sixth,
Defender of the Faith, till lately Emperor of India" by
singing "the national anthem of Mr. Cooke."

The visitors were appalled at this audacity, even
more when Mencken added without a smile, "Of the
London *Daily Worker*, that is." (Mencken knew very
well that at that point I had been a citizen for seven
years, but he trusted to my sporting awareness of the
fact that an Englishman naturalized in America must
in his own lifetime resign himself to be thought a
renegade in his native country, a British spy in his
adopted one.) The Minnesota Youth were stung to
their principles. Only that night, Wallace himself had
described the proper Progressive image of Britain as an
imperialist beast. The leader folded his arms and
conveyed by the swelling veins in his neck that this was
the end. But Mencken assumed they were part of the
choir, and after much coaxing some of them joined in.
What finished them were the lines "Long to-oo reig-
eig-n over us,/Go-odd save the King!" Mencken was
probably the only man there who knew any other
verses, and he wanted to go on with it. "How's it go?"
he blandly asked. "'Scatter his enemies, confound their
knavish tricks'?"

They were exhausted by now and raised their
standard, nodded a casual acknowledgment of the
food and drink, and barged out as noisily as they had
come in. The reader will appreciate, from the personal
memory of similar brawls, that however mild this joke

may read on paper, it was a hilarious end to a great occasion. As they stomped off down the corridor, we groaned and bellowed. Mencken restored his stogie to his mouth and sat down and wiped the happy tears from his eyes with a blue handkerchief.

It was my last memory of him as a happy, whole Mencken. On Good Friday morning of 1955, almost seven years after these happenings and his stroke, I went down to Baltimore to see him. His body had slumped at the middle and his face was a little drawn, but when he came to the door, the gas jet eyes flared for a second and then expired into a watery smile. I noticed that one eye had a drooping lid. He was clearly embarrassed by his physical decline but not for long. We went out into the dooryard for a breath or two of a beautiful spring morning, and two miniature heads bobbed up over the wall. They were the neighbor's children, and they piped, as in a nursery rhyme, "Mister Men-cken, Mis-ter Men-cken." He waved at them and shouted, "Hi, there, rascals."

We went in, and he poured me a short nip of Scotch, remarking, as he might have done to his confessor, that "it was always my drink, you know. They made a big fuss over the beer swilling." I was relieved to notice that whatever parts of the brain had been switched off, the ones that coined his inimitable way of talk were still active. I wondered how he felt about various politicians he had been unable to write about, and frankly called off names in the hope of carrying away some terse characterizations. I was not disappointed. Eisenhower? "Well, for a soldier, he's better than Grant. That's not saying much but, after all, we might have been landed with—what's his name?" He had trouble with some names, and I guessed Stevenson. "Oh, my God, yes: another crooner." And how about the great Roman, General Douglas MacArthur? "MacArthur? He's a dreadful old fraud, but he appears to be fading satisfactorily."

It was he who brought up the Wallace evening, and he cackled again over the thought of the jumpy little man still bickering by correspondence with Rhoda over finance capitalism, to say nothing of her possible relations with me. We went on to other things. He asked how the food was these days at Luchow's, and that brought on memories of various literati of the *Smart Set* days, and of his particular affection for Edgar Lee Masters. He talked of him in the past tense, and I asked him how long Masters had been dead. He was puzzled for a moment, and I suggested something like 1948. "Yeah," said Mencken with no guile at all, "that's right, I believe he died the year I did."

IV

ADLAI
STEVENSON
The Failed Saint

LOS BANOS, CALIFORNIA, is not a place name that
springs readily to the mind even of a presidential
candidate, who must, in the interminable safari of his
campaign, drop in on hundreds of small towns
recommended by county chairmen and other local
scouts and bone up, an hour or two before his arrival,
on their vital statistics, folklore, and means of
livelihood. Nobody was more conscientious, or
panicky, at doing this than Adlai Stevenson. By the
time he had come to California, for what everybody
figures would be the decisive primary of 1956, he was a
ragged but still blithe campaigner. The Florida
primary was yet to be dealt with, and the day he drove
out of San Francisco south and east the 130 miles to
Los Banos, he had prepared for Florida so well that he
had to push into the back of his mind reams of statistics
about old-age pensions, citrus crops, the beef-cattle
industry, and the plight of the Seminoles before he

could begin to memorize the special contributions to civilization of Los Banos, a town of about 6,000 on the eastern rim of the 300-mile roasting pan of the San Joaquin Valley, which ripens half the fruits and nuts a rich nation could desire and, with the help of piped-in water, yields seven or eight crops of alfalfa a year.

By the time we were through the Livermore Valley, Stevenson had taken in such gross statistics and was answering a catechism thrown at him by a native Californian, the head—as I recall—of the Northern California Democrats. "The national" (or as we should now say the ethnic) "composition of the Central Valley?" Long-settled Yankees, Mexicans, and Armenians. "Very good, stress the Armenians. Main source of income?" Cattle, farm implements, fruit. "Right, what fruits?" Oranges...? "Oh God, no, oranges are way to the south; peaches, peaches, peaches, you don't have to mention much else, the whole valley is known as the Peach Bowl, they pack and can seventy-two million quarts of fruit a year, stay with the peaches and the canning, and for God's sake don't forget irrigation." Stevenson carried a black leather-bound loose-leaf notebook, like an economics professor on the way to a lecture, and he scribbled inserts in it with the guilty air of a bright-eyed schoolboy who is just a shade behind on his homework.

The choice of Los Banos was not a haphazard stab at a map, not one of those condescending excursions to a rural outpost out of which the news agencies might pluck a phrase or two that would cheer the farmers. Stevenson's last rival for the nomination, Senator Estes Kefauver, had chosen to go there before the Stevenson men. Los Banos was the packing center for the fruit canners. More important, it was the site of the Merced County spring fair and livestock show. And

136

that year, the fair would come to its climax on
Mother's Day. The Stevenson men got wind of the fact
that Kefauver would appear in Los Banos on that very
day, no doubt to dispense his finest brand of Davy
Crockett homespun charm and simple sense. Stevenson put in a bid to appear, too, and the Mayor of Los
Banos resolved what might have been a sticky feud by
inviting both candidates to speak in turn, in what he
hoped would pass imperishably into the books as the
Democrats' one and only attempt at a Lincoln-
Douglas Debate.

From June to November the sun blazes like a
fireball over the Central Valley. It was mid-May now,
but soon after dawn it was hot and dry, and as the
parade came jogging in from the horizon at the far end
of the main street, even the marchers and the wheels of
the floats kicked up puffs of dust that rose like smoke
signals into a cloudless sky. Along the sidewalks, the
people were stacked like dolls and blobs of costume
jewelry in a toy-store window, most of the women in
purple or emerald shirts (the Mexican mania), and red,
green, or yellow pedal pushers, the men in denim slacks
or jeans. Little cheers followed the puffs of dust as the
drum majorettes, the band, the creaking floats came
on. The big item was a courtly group of local beauties,
all frills and teeth and grins pinned from ear to ear,
sedately erect in giant papier-mâché ice-cream cones.
After this masterpiece, a blonde rode alone. She was
Miss Merced County of 1956. Behind her came her
esquire, or knight-at-arms, on a high-stepping straw-
berry roan. He was a Humpty Dumpty little man
in bursting blue jeans, a denim coat with lampshade
tassels flapping from the shoulder pads, a red string tie,
and surmounting his small red balloon of a face a ten-
gallon hat.

The parade had built up and slowed down at one intersection, and Humpty Dumpty reined in his horse and looked down, like an exhausted sheriff, at a tall city slicker in an uncommonly well-cut Swiss silk suit, who was crumpling the paper from a good twenty-cent cigar. The slicker looked up at him with a satisfied grin. "Hi, Adlai," said the slicker, "how you feelin'?"

"Hullo, Estes," said Humpty Dumpty, "I'm fine, I guess. A little tired, though."

"Same with me," said Senator Kefauver, jamming the cigar between his lips and giving off the expansive air of a man suddenly refreshed. The parade moved on, with the comic, forlorn Stevenson bouncing after it. Kefauver peered out of the crowd and watched him depart with immense satisfaction. Kefauver had gone up and down the land in his coonskin cap, mouthing his folksy greetings from the snows of New Hampshire to the docks of San Diego. For this one day, he had decided to rest up from his Davy Crockett tour. He was a famous clown on his day off: the dressy, sane civilian. He had appeared as such, waving and walking, earlier on. The Mayor had advertised that he would set up applause meters to check the relative popularity of the two candidates. Whoever got the most applause would have the privilege of choosing to speak first or last on the fairgrounds in the afternoon.

The meters, for some never-explained reason, would not work "in the open air" (the Mayor said). So the two campaign managers were reduced to the flip of a coin. Adlai won and, with characteristic naiveté, chose to speak first.

Before the great debate, there was a break for lunch. Stevenson came into the tent reserved for his camp. He was panting in the noonday sun and slapping his forehead. "Get me out," he said, "of this ridiculous costume." He went off somewhere and got himself into a suit that was meant to banish forever, but didn't, the memory of his woeful impersonation of a B-film sheriff. This was his last attempt to accommodate all the nagging politicos along the way who had urged him to relax the Stevenson austerity and rough up the Stevenson wit. He had been dogged since the start of the 1956 campaign by the warnings and tips of the "image" makers. They had kept tabs on Kefauver's ubiquitous folksiness. On the verge of the California primary, they had tapped the polls and warned Stevenson of something called "Kefauver's superior electability." Los Banos was meant to be a jolting demonstration of it.

Stevenson shoveled a lunch of ham and beans and potato salad off a cardboard plate; plastic chicken or *haute cuisine* was all the same to the wolfing Stevenson, who—in another tent in Iowa a few years later—would prove that a patrician Princetonian could easily outwolf the peasant Khrushchev with minutes to spare.

Then he walked across the stubble of the fairgrounds and stood up on a rudimentary platform. I chose to stay close by Kefauver, who stood under the shade of a pepper tree and watched. It was an unsettling time for Adlai, who, while he was being introduced, was scribbling away in his London School of Economics notebook, jotting down a figure, adding no doubt a last-minute snatch of the Book of Job. For a minute or two, Adlai's bright cracks drew nothing but a puzzled silence from the lolling and stretched-out farmers, and heedless somersaults from their innumerable children on the grass.

At last he got down to his notebook and started to mourn for the valley farmer, whose $185 cow now sold for $175; for alarming unemployment in the farm-implement business; for farmers everywhere "paying

139

an unfair and a serious price for their efficiency, for their success"; for the Republican habit of "dedicating dams after the Democrats had built them"; for the outrageous lack of water in valleys that could "richly use" the flow of the West's great rivers. He apologized for not attacking the Secretary of Agriculture, "more out of respect for the Sabbath than for the Secretary."

He had been advised, as a working rule for the California campaign, to stick to local issues and make, if possible, one grammatical error a day. He couldn't do it. It was an impossible prescription for a civilized man, and though he did his best and pictured the Eisenhower administration as "a-stumblin' and a-fallin'" whenever it dealt with the farmer, he sounded like a facetious headmaster making a last-ditch effort to be one of his boys. He was going on and on, well beyond the agreed ten-minute limit, and a State Senator, a Democrat, who had agreed to serve as timekeeper, stood up below the platform and helped Stevenson not at all by making slicing motions across his neck to indicate it was time to stop.

Stevenson glanced at the notebook once again, got off a biblical quotation, about "the fruit of the waters of the Lord," that baffled everybody. As a final quip, he produced a newspaper clipping. It was, from the Sacramento *Bee*, a tart little editorial blasting farm subsidies and their recipients as "parasites."

"Well," cried the irrepressible Adlai, "I am a farmer too, and I say to you, my fellow parasites..."

"What did he call us?" muttered a farmer close by Kefauver's pepper tree. Kefauver smiled. Adlai bowed to lackadaisical clapping, stepped down, and shook the wan hand of a circus clown and was gone. Now it was Kefauver's turn.

He stood in the broiling sun with his neck as stiff as a turkey's, and the gray wings of his hair neatly curled.

Well, friends, this was Mother's Day, and a Sunday, and not the time or place for a partisan speech. He spent about twenty seconds on the Republicans' callousness about new dams, and said he was one who wanted to see water, water everywhere. But enough of politics. He just wanted to say he had seen some great sportin' events in his time but never finer athletes anywhere than in the sports events in that valley over the weekend. He also had seen fine children in his day, but watching the parade, he decided "I never saw more beautiful children in my life." Incidentally, incidentally, my friends, he had never seen a more impressive parade, "anywhere, at any time." A tidal wave of cheers. He modulated into a reverent drone about the beauty of motherhood. The main thing was never to forget that the spirit of Mother's Day "is one of compassion, and if we could get that message across to the world, why, ah think everythin' would be all right." He ended with a line worthy of Eatanswill or Mark Twain: "I would like to end right there, and then step among you and shake your hands. I would like to pay a humble tribute to those of you *who have lost fine mothers!*"

There is surely nobody alive who would take the risk of publicly proclaiming, on Mother's Day, that he had lost a lousy mother. Everybody in Los Banos thought of Mom in her grave. The farmers nodded or grunted; the women dabbed their eyes or banged the palms of their hands. Kefauver stepped down, like one of the disciples, and did indeed press every hand in sight. The mystery of his "superior electability" seemed a mystery no more, at least in the rural counties.

Well, Kefauver lost the primary, and the Democratic nomination. But if the 1956 California primary was not Stevenson's Waterloo, as the Kefauverites had confidently predicted, it was his

Austerlitz: the last brilliant battle won before the signs appeared that the war itself was about to close in on him. Now he was left to the long campaign against the champ, Eisenhower himself. I suspect he had more than an inkling of the seriousness of this prospect on the night of the California primary when the returns came flooding in. In midevening, I went over to Kefauver's headquarters, where in a small hotel suite the Senator was greeting everybody with wide grins, handshakes (of course), and clinking glasses. He ducked from time to time into an inner room to watch the returns coming in on the tape. As the news got worse, Kefauver got merrier. At last, when he knew it was all over, he broke out champagne. We got a glimpse of a character quite different from the sanctimonious, careful-treading, achingly folksy Senator from Tennessee. He waved us a happy farewell, his glasses flashing mischief and good cheer. He was a sporting pro who'd lost. The gambler's Swiss silk suit and rakish cigar did not seem so incongruous, after all.

I went on to Stevenson's suite, downtown in the grander Biltmore. There we should see ecstasy, and Adlai's quips showering on an audience fit to bathe in them. But the place was empty. The Governor had not yet returned from his workers' victory party. There were only three of us, old newspaper friends, and a reporter and a girl photographer from the Los Angeles *Times*. We went up to a floor in the sky and were shown into a large, funereal gothic suite, with a suggestion of ramparts and slots for archers on the terrace: the sort of pad you would expect William Randolph Hearst to have kept for brief sojourns out of San Simeon.

We sat and waited, and just when we guessed that Stevenson might be about to arrive on the shoulders of a crowd in a torchlight procession, he came bustling in, alone, muttering apologies. We offered handshakes and congratulations, and he accepted them with a grave face and a bowed head, as if he had just endured his first communion. There was no quippery, no laughter, and incidentally, no champagne, no beer, nothing to wet a whistle. After a rather awkward interlude, more like a confessional, in which he said something about gratitude and humility, he got up briskly, apologized for his tiredness, and showed us out. In this surprising wake, I got the impression also that he knew the mock battles were over and ahead of him stretched the grind of the campaign against—he admitted it later on—the undefeatable Eisenhower. Eisenhower did not have to pretend to be the quintessential American, of which Stevenson would be required to go on giving such an amateur theatrical parody. Eisenhower was the thing itself. It was another and enlightening example of the dependable fatuity of public relations experts when confronted by defeat: instead of taking a cool second look at the elements of a client's character that might arouse a new appeal, they begin to invent or rejig an "image" as close as possible to the one that seems to be working for the opposition.

After the 1952 defeat, I sat with Stevenson late one night in the Governor's mansion in Springfield. It was the first time I had seen him since the election, and at last we got round to the hard facts of why he'd lost. The inevitable tendency of all such post-mortems is to weave a self-justifying cloak of rationalizations, hindsight discoveries of false techniques. It was one of the heartening, and always startling, things about Stevenson that he could pierce this sort of fustian with a single touch of candor. He leaned back and grinned and said, "Who did I think I was, running against George Washington?" Four years later, when he'd lost again, I sent him a cryptic telegram: "How now?" To which, overnight, came the reply: "Who did I think I was running against George Washington twice?" Months after that, cheerfully resigned to another life, as he insisted, he one night started to make an honest show of concern for the Democratic Party and began to speculate on the likely next nominee. There was something deliberately manly about this high-minded talk which made me suspect that he had not absolutely renounced the Holy Grail. I said, "Governor, what you have to worry about is not 1960 but 1964." He gave me that look of eyepopping alarm which he held in reserve for questions to which he feared he ought to know the answer, or books he felt he ought to have read. (I got the impression that he never read any books at all but skimmed very rapidly through recommended tomes in the guilty hope that one day he would have time. He would never have time.)

Well, I said, remember William Jennings Bryan: "nominated in 1896, beaten, nominated again in 1900, beaten, then given up for lost in 1904 and passed over in favor of the dazzling Alton B. Parker, when—presto!—1908 and they go for Bryan again—again he's beaten." Oddly, he did not laugh or pooh-pooh it. "Tell me more," he said.

And, sure enough, there was embarrassing proof, in 1960, that once a man is X-rayed for the presidency, he is radioactive into his paltering old age. In December, 1959, the Democrats threw a big dinner at the Waldorf-Astoria in New York which was intended as a tribute to Averell Harriman, Harry Truman's failed candidate in 1956. At least eight Democrats already panting for the party nomination came up to the rostrum and gave their rhetorical all. But it was Adlai who stampeded the ballroom. In the flush of this resurrection, he retired to his tent, and announced that he would make no effort toward the nomination. He would wait, like Caesar, for the third offer. The imperial gesture enraged the Kennedys, who, throughout the most politically sensitive of 3000 counties, had been nursing a legion of convention delegates. That same night, the Kennedy camp sent a courier (from John F. Kennedy's hot denial to me that he had ever gone to see Stevenson, it was irresistible to infer that the messenger was his brother Robert) to say to Stevenson, in the gutty version confirmed by two onlookers, that the Kennedys had worked their tails off for Stevenson in 1952 and 1956, and if he would not now reciprocate, they had no intention of working their tails off for themselves only to "hand the nomination to you on a platter" if the Kennedy push failed at the convention. From then on, the camaraderie between the Kennedys and Stevenson was cool at best. Yet the brothers and their team kept a wary eye on him and in public were at all times respectful this side of reverence. For they greatly feared a standoff at the convention between their own forces and those of the wily Texan Senator Lyndon B. Johnson, and there was always the possibility that Stevenson back from Elba might be able to muster an army not big enough to win but big enough to choose the winner. It never happened, and Stevenson's final sulk in his Los Angeles tent was as revealing as anything he had done in the previous campaigns of a trait in his character fatal to his ambitions as a winning politician.

Two days before Kennedy was nominated at Los Angeles, the masters of the Pennsylvania, New York, Michigan, and Illinois delegations came to Stevenson and begged him to announce that he was in the running. They assured him that the Kennedys' hold on the convention could be broken. They were hardy veterans of state and convention politics. Together, they could command an incomparable block of convention votes. It would have been hard to pick four men at Los Angeles more qualified to engineer a stampede. All they asked was an announcement by Stevenson that he was, after all and in the last stretch, a candidate. He would not do it. He paced the room. On the one hand, perhaps. On the other hand, perhaps not. In the end, he refused. He continued to hope for some Garfield eruption of sentiment on the floor that would precipitate the blushing Adlai to the rostrum, where—as at Chicago in 1952—it might be recorded that he, "saying he would ne'er consent, consented."

That, of course, never happened either. But on the day before the nomination, Stevenson committed the ultimate gaffe. He came into the hall as an innocent delegate obediently joining his brothers from Illinois. He expected, and received, a buoyant cry from the doors, then a cheer, then a pounding wave of cheers; and he went up to the rostrum, thanked them all for "a tumultuous and moving welcome" and dribbled off into facetiae implying that he could sense the way the wind was blowing and was happy not to be caught in the draft. The men of Texas and Massachusetts stood with faces like slabs of cement, livid at a precedent that finished forever the old rule of taste and prudence which forbade candidates ever to appear in the convention hall before their nomination (as late as Wendell Willkie's time—1940—the rule was never to appear in the convention *city*. Willkie was such a novice that he had never heard of it, and showed up in Philadelphia anyway).

On the morning of Kennedy's nomination, Stevenson's small and now frantic band of campaigners recruited—at $2 a soldier—a guerrilla force of students, idealists, onlookers, slaphappy beatniks and fitted them out with posters ("America Needs Stevenson," "We Dig Adlai"), hoisting which they dribbled down to the Sports Arena and harassed and mocked the early delegates. By midafternoon, when the convention was in sitting order, the Stevenson mob threatened to storm the doors. Extra police came tumbling in and kept the sans-culottes plodding in circles till the sun went down, when the doors were opened to them and they marched freely in. Their chanted slogans were intended to reinforce the contention of the Stevenson managers that he had several million idolaters in California alone. But he also had 31½ delegates, no more. Kennedy had 785. It was a vain and shabby end to a romance that had started eight years before in Chicago, when the Governor of Illinois rose to make the usual formal address of welcome to the delegates and, after no more than ten minutes' exposure of his extraordinary grace, eloquence, and wit, turned into the plumed knight himself, waiting to be taken and given the supreme command.

One week after these humiliations, Stevenson was at home in Libertyville and, it may be supposed, had willingly purged himself of all further lust for power. I went to spend a day of blistering heat with him, and at first sight he was thoroughly recovered, a blithe, even comic character, walking around his inferno of a living room in an open Truman shirt braying with donkeys, a pair of sandals, and binding shorts no bigger than a bikini. A jokey mention of 1964, and the footsteps of William Jennings Bryan, had him bubbling with chuckles and self-deprecating asides. But he was, for a retired statesman on a sweltering day, puzzlingly jumpy. He fussed with papers, marched off for drinks, came bobbing in—his shape, so scantily disguised, was that of a big toy Schmoo—whenever he heard the telephone ring. In time, he slumped into an armchair, cocked an ankle on a plump thigh, and began to fret aloud. He was by no means about to decline into an elder of the party. He was not done with politics, not with government, anyway. There had been dirty work in Los Angeles which was at once too complicated and humiliating to go into. He rambled on, with considerable asperity, in a way I had never known. He was practically free-associating without thought of an audience. He was, in fact, waiting for the telephone to ring. This came out obliquely, through a wayward maze of reminiscences of his childhood, his luck in seeing bigwigs on visits to his grandfather, Vice President Stevenson, his meeting Woodrow Wilson, his father's service in the Navy Department under Josephus Daniels, his attendance as a boy at both a Republican and a Bull Moose convention. The general implication was that he had been heir to a political tradition and he was in it for life.

And how did the Kennedys figure in prolonging it? That was the rub of his anxiety. The Kennedys had less cause than ever to feel any obligation to him, but a week had gone by and feuds dissipate, and by now "the young man" (he kept calling him) must be thinking about his Cabinet. Whether he was or not, it became suddenly very clear, Stevenson was thinking about nothing but the State Department. He began to assemble the points for an argument that would lead inevitably to his appointment as Secretary of State. (This, he now maintained, had always been his prime ambition. He had even had it in mind when, in 1948, he expected to be adopted by the Cook County Democratic leader as the Democrats' nominee for Senator. Stevenson had been aglow with visions of soaring speeches in the Senate, a fantasy at first encouraged and then rudely punctured by Jake Arvey, the Cook County boss. The Repbulicans were putting up a war hero as their senatorial choice, and Arvey decided that Paul Douglas, a Marine hero, would be a better match for him. Arvey also suspected, like everybody else except Harry Truman, that 1948 was to be a Republican year and that the Illinois governorship was a lost cause. If Douglas won the Senate seat, and Stevenson lost, Arvey could maintain his *amour-propre* by saying he had at least picked a "classy" type for Governor who was innocent of all malodorous political connections. In any case, to Stevenson's anguish, Arvey phoned him and simply told him he was going to be Governor, while Paul Douglas had been chosen "to go international." Stevenson was given twenty-four hours before filing day to accept the switch. By his own painful account, he went into his usual back-and-forth trot and oscillated between humble acceptance and proud rejection until the telephone rang at the deadline and he caved in before an Arvey harangue.)

Secretary of State. That was it. I glanced across the room at the only other person present at this ordeal: the Washington columnist Marquis Childs, an old Stevenson friend. We both knew enough about the temper and prejudices of the Kennedy brain trust to be certain that Stevenson would never be on the list of suggested Secretaries of State. At this point, Stevenson closed the door of his study and, sensing (I suppose) our misgivings, asked us frankly to tot up good reasons why he might not be the choice. After several polite feints at avoiding the obvious, we compiled a roster of damning reasons beginning with the nasty encounter at the Waldorf-Astoria the previous December (which Stevenson had forgotten!) and ending with reminders of the implacable enmity toward him of men most powerful in the Kennedy entourage. These included most especially John Bailey, Kennedy's chief political broker and front man in practically every state of the

Union, and the whole camp of Kennedy's Boston buddies who were to turn into the kitchen cabinet and be known as "the Irish Mafia"; their city-bred distrust of him as the haughty lord lieutenant of the county had been whipped into something between amusement and contempt by what they considered the Stevenson treachery at Los Angeles. Even old Jim Farley, Roosevelt's kingmaker, who had stood outside the battle as a retired field marshal, had been cheered by the Kennedy team for remarking, "If you want your appeasement candidate, there he is," after Stevenson had bitterly condemned American U-2 reconnaissance flights over the Soviet Union—in a speech at Oxford University that was greatly praised by the European press. ("The trouble with me," said Stevenson, "is I always run on the wrong continent.")

All this Childs and I had to put tentatively, careful not to hurt his feelings, as if we were offering wise reasons why he should not take a position he had already been offered. But the cumulative reminders of so much distaste and actual opposition apparently convinced him that the telephone would ring. He got up from his chair and padded around the room in his ridiculous beach costume, twirling his glasses on one of their wings. He grunted and then said a remarkable thing, the sort of line no dramatist could write: "And, to think—I've known *this kid* for twenty years." It was the only mean thing I ever heard him say, about anybody. He could resent criticism, but not for long; he could flinch and say nothing before vicious attacks; he could often sigh and concede the possible justice in hard things said about him. Only once did I hear him say, "He is, I think, the only human being I have ever truly hated." (The year was 1956; he was talking about Vice President Richard M. Nixon.) But snideness and malice were beyond him. In the moment of saying "this kid," his bluebottle eyes bulged, and he quickly changed his tone and said, "So, then, what d'you think it's to be?" Not for a moment, it seemed, did he suppose he would be wholly overlooked. Not for himself so much as for the millions of his faithful, the Kennedys would find something dignified and safe.

We suggested this and that, took a high-flying, flattering guess at the Supreme Court, and I remember venting a passing thought which I regretted the moment it emerged as a sound: "Maybe they'll decide to put you out to pasture at the United Nations." He did not take too kindly to the thought put that way, but when the offer came, of course, he took it. And his faithful flock was revived by the prospect of Stevenson, the new elder statesman, addressing a world forum with uncommon eloquence and sincerity, expressing the best of America, a standing symbol of probity and high ideals among the petty strife and wheeler-dealing of the international marketplace. To the extent that Stevenson himself shared, however modestly, this view of his role in the United Nations he deluded himself about the function of an ambassador and blotted out the uneasy knowledge that he had indeed been chosen as the dressiest possible salesman for policies, good and dubious, that the Kennedy administration had to offer.

He learned early, to his chagrin, that he was not to be the sole or even chief drafter of American speeches before the UN. It was hard for him to accept what career men know from the start, that an ambassador is a courier or channel of policy and not its inventor. The more he was able to accept this subordinate part, the more he tried to compensate for his disillusion by making the most of his social gifts, as a delightful host, among the delegations, among the representatives of what was called the Third World especially. This was an exercise in civility and goodwill that will not be set down in the records of the United Nations or any of its agencies. But it was a noble and humane effort nonetheless, and the retired or cashiered delegates from many African and Asian nations will not forget it. Some of them came indeed to recall their happiest times in America as those in the Ambassador's regal suite at the Waldorf Towers. These warm memories had the effect, however, even at the time, of spreading the unspoken word that Stevenson was the thoroughly civilized victim of a hard-nosed administration in Washington. In keeping Stevenson marooned in his tower in New York, the Kennedys had not been quite as smart as they thought. And very soon, Stevenson's speeches in the forum itself were seen by the shrewder delegates of the big nations to be rather hollow echoes of his old resounding style. Inevitably, since they were drafted and screened in Washington; the body of the music was written there, and Stevenson was left to put in the cadenzas and fiddly bits.

On his visits to Washington, he discovered that he was politely listened to but his initiative was debarred. He could come back from such chill briefings, obediently devote his days and early evenings to scribbling notes on a score of issues and what the Kennedys liked to call "position papers," and then devote his nights to parties. He was, perhaps had always been, a voracious party man, tonight a buoyant and funny host, tomorrow a willing guest on the hop between three or four old friends, for one of the winning things about him was his loyalty to friends and admiring acquaintances whether famous or obscure. I don't recall his ever turning down an invitation to a brief call, or a drink snatched between a duty dinner and a midnight conference. He tried to work everything in, social fun not least. It was an appetite that did not endear him to all of the UN's bigwigs. On the contrary, it offered more monkish types the excuse of saying that he was frivoling away his great gifts. Dag Hammarskjöld, the Secretary-General, had admired Stevenson the presidential campaigner but came to have little respect for him as a negotiator or even as a well-informed ambassador. Hammarskjöld was a paragon of discretion, as a Secretary-General had better be, but once, in a private place, pressed to say what he thought would be Stevenson's future, he stonily replied, "That man will be ruined by the dowagers."

It should be said that whenever his own convictions coincided with a Kennedy policy, Stevenson was as forceful an advocate in the United Nations as his country could hope for. On supporting the national interests of the Congolese people against the inroads of the Russians; on defending Hammarskjöld against the onslaught of the Soviet Union's proposal to replace the Secretary-General's lone authority with a "troika" in the General Assembly; on attacking apartheid; on defending the rights of neutrals, in the breakup of the African colonies—on these and other issues he felt warmly about he was certainly as effective as any American Ambassador to the UN before or since. But the job itself is a thorn in the flesh of any man with lively ambitions to be a statesman.

The bitterest disillusion, the supreme humiliation of Stevenson's public career, came too early for him to believe that he would never again be at the political helm. In the spring of 1961, when the Kennedy administration was only a few months old, a plan was going forward, in the White House, the Pentagon, and the Central Intelligence Agency, to invade Fidel Castro's Cuba (with which the United States had already broken diplomatic relations) with a force of

Cuban refugees secretly trained by the United States. *The New York Times* had wondered for some time what the American military was doing training Cubans in Guatemala. Only days before the invasion, President Kennedy had given the press his unqualified word that "there will not be, under any conditions, an intervention in Cuba by the United States armed forces." Few people stopped to ask, "By whom, then?" The precise word "intervention" was Kennedy's semantic loophole. The Cubans were, in fact, ferried to their coastline, on the Bay of Pigs, by "United States armed forces" and left to invade and be pulverized.

For weeks before this ghastly ineptitude, the Cubans had been screaming in the United Nations about an imminent "intervention" by the United States. Stevenson mustered some of his most eloquent anger to deny the charge. A day after Kennedy's confirming promise, Cuban air bases were bombed in a softening-up operation. Then came the invasion, and in the smoke and failure of it came a session of the United Nations Political Committee of the Assembly. The Cuban Foreign Minister, Dr. Raul Roa, directly accused the United States government of aggression, and in particular of having dispatched United States military aircraft to bomb Cuba. Two of these planes, riddled by antiaircraft, had limped into Key West and Miami respectively. They bore the markings of Castro's Air Force. The one that landed at Miami Airport was photographed by the press, and the local immigration director read a statement, supposedly in the pilot's words, to the effect that he was only one of four who had defected from Castro's Air Force and used the stolen planes to help the invaders.

Stevenson was well prepared for his rebuttal. After reiterating, in his most resonant oratorical manner, Kennedy's promise about nonintervention, he stabbed out the confident sentences: "No United States personnel participated. No United States aircraft of any kind participated. These two planes, to the best of our knowledge, were Castro's own Air Force planes, and according to the pilots, they took off from Castro's own Air Force fields." To prove it, Stevenson had a photographic blowup of one of the wounded planes. He pointed to the Cuban star, and the revolutionary Air Force initials, on the tail. He ended with a brisk and righteous peroration, declaring again that Cuban refugees alone had carried the invasion and adding that the United States was far too proud and honorable a power to stoop to such sneaky deceptions as Dr. Roa had charged.

The speech left a vast television audience with a relieved feeling of gratitude that Adlai Stevenson on that day had been the spokesman for American honor. When the meeting recessed for lunch, Stevenson had a congratulatory phone call from the White House. He went into the dining room to a rustle of admiration from the surrounding tables. Delegates came over and shook his hand, and he bobbed up and blushed and was "very grateful." By that time, however, Kennedy had sent flying into New York one of his closest advisers, who came on to the United Nations, buttonholed Stevenson as he came out of lunch, and said to him simply, "The President thinks you ought to know *it was our show*"! But the planes, the markings? The markings had been faked by the CIA and the photograph passed on to Stevenson to bolster the official case. When Stevenson heard later, whether it was true or not, that he was known in the White House as "our official liar," his self-esteem was at its nadir.

Only a few days later, he came round for a drink and—since, like everybody else, I had accepted his UN speech as a rousing and comforting defense—I was not disturbed to see him as bustling and cheerful as ever. A very small incident has preserved itself in my memory as a fixed association with the Bay of Pigs. I had gone off into the pantry to make the drinks, with the help of my twelve-year-old daughter, who had worshiped Adlai from afar and was in a dither of joy at having finally seen him in the flesh. About that flesh I had had mildly jocose things to say in the past. In some profile or other I had once described him as having "a bosun's roll," implying both his hobbling gait and the innuendo of a spare tire. Whenever he had put on an extra pound or two, which he often alarmed himself by doing overnight, he would pat his middle and wonder how the bosun's roll was doing. My daughter, in a deafening stage whisper, said to me, "My God, Daddy, you were right about the bosun's roll." From the living room there rang out a merry tenor: "You can say that again, Susie." She gave a voiceless scream and vanished, never—I think—to come near him again.

His laugh chased her down a corridor and into her room. There was no call to apologize for her to such a friend, who enjoyed mischief in others as much as he did in himself. I anticipated a happy visit and the chance of offering him straightforward congratulations on his United Nations speech, something it was not always easy to do, for I was one of those who was, more often than not, made uncomfortable by speeches and lectures (his Godkin Lectures at Harvard were a prime example) that were invariably eloquent and noble but tantalizingly vague about what to do here and now. In fact, I have to admit that much, if not most, of Stevenson's political thought adds up to a makeshift warning to avoid all quick solutions while trusting, in the meantime, to a general outbreak of courage, tolerance, compassion, and universal brotherhood. His view of "the people" was always a brave one, but in its blindness to the effective cunning, bigotry, and deviousness of a good many of the 200 million people any President has to deal with, it was not much more realistic than Carl Sandburg's maudlin apostrophes to "The Pee-pul Yes" of the prairies. This is not to belittle Stevenson's speaking style, unique in our time, and the sense it always conveyed of one gallant and civilized man speaking for himself and not, as most of his predecessors and successors, for a chorus of invisible ghosts. But the longer I knew him, the more I felt that all the essential mechanisms of politics—the money raising, the reconciliation of obnoxious opposites, the hurly-burly of party machines, the need to accommodate the grosser needs of a community to its idealistic hopes, if any—were looked on, by him, as concessions to defeat. He was essentially a moral spokesman, "a good man," as Mencken said of Grover Cleveland, "in a bad trade." As such, he was a setup for the role the crafty Kennedys had groomed him for: the noble cat's-paw.

When the laughter was over, I handed him his drink and congratulated him on the splendid speech in the UN. I remember now the deliberate way he put down his drink, adjusted his tie, put the tips of his chubby fingers together, and looked away from me into the far corner of the room with an expression halfway between shame and despair. He said, "I have something very dreadful to tell you." And then it all came out. He had been well briefed about the Cuban charges. He had known, and felt uneasy, about the training of Cuban volunteers in Guatemala (Kennedy himself had learned about it—from the CIA—only a week or two after he was elected). Something, Stevenson was given to understand, was in the wind. But the White House had convinced him that any invasion would be an adventure of the Cuban refugees done on their own initiative, without any sort of help from the United States. He accepted in complete good faith the faked photograph handed to him by the CIA.

What to do? As always, he did not deign to recriminate or relieve his bitterness in a drone of complaints or abuse. But he was at the end of his rope politically—or so I imagined. I should have known him better. I thought he was pondering the least damaging way to resign. I was not simple enough to believe that he would ever want to quit the game of power, at least the appearance of being in it. But what he appeared to be fishing for was a dignified out that would not close the door on his later reentry. I reminded him that "there was once a conservative in England who quit in good conscience and, if anything, took on a new stature." The stress on "conservative" must have been a Freudian slip, but a true one. I was talking about Anthony Eden. Stevenson was at once glum and astonished. He had not been thinking at all about resignation. It was very early in the Kennedy administration. He would surely be burning his boats once and for all. So he would, I said. But even in this moment of total humiliation, he had nowhere to go but the corridors, if not the seats, of power. The law bored him acutely. And there was never any more than wistful daydreaming in his frequent declarations that he would love to retire, like Robert E. Lee, to some small college to read and teach wisely and be pointed out as a great and good man who had done the state some service. The truth is that Adlai Stevenson was a man in whom ambition never ceased to palpitate. He had come to seek friendly comfort and sympathy, not a life decision.

Nothing was resolved—I am sure he saw scores of sympathetic friends at that time, enough of them to bolster his secret hope that he could stay on at the

United Nations and keep his self-respect. Which, surprisingly, he did. More surprising still, to anyone who had taken a cool look at the facts of the Cuban adventure, President Kennedy—when all the fumbling chicanery of it was out in the open—had increased his own standing in the popularity polls.

Stevenson turned quickly to cheerier matters, said he must be going, and stopped to look at a Staffordshire statuette, standing on my piano, which depicts an auburn-haired dandy in an aubergine cloak sitting astride a show horse got up with ceremonial trappings. He must have seen it before, but now he caught its inscription. He bent down and squinted at it. It said: "A. Lincoln." Nothing but the truth, I said; it was Lincoln as a circuit rider. Stevenson fingered the cloak and glanced uneasily at two little blobs of rouge on the cheeks. "If he'd ever appeared in Illinois like that, they'd have run him out of the state," he said, and whinnied with laughter. Which was an improvement on what he had once told me about his experience with another Lincoln artifact. It was that evening in the White House when he had finally yielded to Harry Truman's beseechings to run for the Democratic nomination in 1952. He was put in the Lincoln Room. When he came to undress, he looked at the bed, he looked at the prints on the wall, he shuffled around the bed, staring at it in awe. He could not bring himself to lie in it. He bedded down on the sofa. I don't know if he was ever apprised of the catch: in Lincoln's day the bed wasn't there, the sofa was.

WHATEVER CHARITABLE RATIONALIZATIONS are brought to bear on his last years, I cannot believe that the Bay of Pigs disaster was anything but the end for him. And in those years, seeing him in his activism in the United Nations, or in his anecdotage at private parties, one had to raise a private cheer for the old campaigner who was not quite a campaigner, for the greatly ambitious man born, as someone said, to lose the presidency. He repaid the Kennedy treachery with tedious hard work, obedient loyalty to the White House, unfailing courtesy and good humor to the delegates of over 100 nations whether they were distinguished, fractious, or banal.

In those years, I think he finally came to accept the bad memories with the good. He was getting into his middle sixties, and there was no possible hope of advancement. He was able, one vivid time, to make an evening out of a rundown of his many humiliations at the hands of his party's leaders, like a retired vaudevillian recalling with zest the time he was booed off the stage, the time he fell into the trombone.

There was the first time, when Truman fetched him in from Illinois to tell him he was first choice for President. How Stevenson had gone through his characteristic minuet, deferring, retreating, bowing, advancing, retreating again, till Truman exploded: "Adlai, you're the most indecisive man I ever met!" It was the beginning of the Hamlet legend, and though it has been exemplified and scorned in a hundred stories, it was true enough. My own most disturbing proof of it came late one night in the Springfield mansion when he was packing to make way for a new Governor. We had been reminiscing and burying the first campaign, and about two in the morning he got up and, I assumed, was off to bed. No, he had a little business to attend to in his study, but it would take ten minutes or so and we could go on from there. Anyway, he said with a weary smile, "sleep is something I'm not very good at." If he was tired at midnight, he took a pill and woke around two. He tossed a little, skimmed a memo or some clippings, took another pill, and struggled out of the pit at seven. The "business" he had to attend to was an unsung tale of the McCarthy time. A young woman, a secretary in the State Health Commission, had been advertised, by some nosy group, as having Communist connections. She had been hounded with threatening letters; state legislators had questioned her right to hold her job; in the end her troubles had wound up on the Governor's desk. Stevenson had gone into it and found that some remote relative, a second cousin or so, had once been engaged to or known, or was said to have known, a fellow who was "reputed to" belong to a Communist front. Stevenson had written here, there, and everywhere attesting to her competence and "loyalty." But the rumors and charges would not down. He had yet another letter to write, and he pulled out of a drawer a fat file, on nothing but the unhappy lady. He wrote his note, sighed, and put the file back. I asked him casually how long this had been going on. "About two years," he said. From his account of it, I could only feel touched by his patience but amazed that he had not, at some early stage, blasted the accusers, confirmed the woman in her job, and moved on to other matters. He was still fretting, if not temporizing, about it. This, it struck me, was not Franklin Roosevelt, lighting a cigarette and telling some underling to reinstate the woman and put an end to it. This was not Harry Truman, weighing the contradictory estimates of American losses in an invasion of the Japanese islands, ordering up the atomic bomb, and going off into a dreamless sleep. This was not Winston Churchill, coming out of a sound short night in one of the dreadful dawns after Dunkirk, zipping up his siren suit, and saying with a grin; "Where are the Nah-ziz?" It was immensely to Stevenson's credit that he had spent two years not letting the matter drop. But the fact that his concern went flickering on in his conscience and never exploded into a burst of anger, or a final decision, suggested a President too sensitive, if not for this world, certainly for this Republic.

There was the time when a rumor started to sprout, during the first campaign, that Stevenson was a homosexual. It disturbed one State Senator, a Republican friend, sufficiently to have him come up to the mansion and go into it at breakfast. The man was embarrassed when he saw me behind a plate of scrambled eggs, but Stevenson assured him first that the rumor was old stuff and secondly that I was present not as a reporter. I mention it now, as a reporter, because it was clear as could be from Stevenson's serene and amused air in listening to this anxious graybeard that he was long familiar with a burden that all public men who are bachelors or divorced have to bear. Stevenson, speaking through chomping mouthfuls of the eggs, the bacon, the sausage, and the toast, told how the rumor had got to New Orleans when he was about to address a meeting of party regulars; how Speaker Sam Rayburn had come in from Texas, assembled the group before Stevenson appeared, and said simply, "You better be careful from now on with such talk: Governor Stevenson was a recruit in the You-Nited States Marines!" The meeting had cowered into respectful silence. "And you know something?" said Stevenson. "It wasn't the Marines, it was the Naval Reserve—for a month or two." He sat back and roared. And the anxious Senator went off, enormously relieved.

There was the time when Stevenson arrived in Chicago for the 1956 convention and heard the bombshell of Harry Truman's decision to renounce him and back Averell Harriman for President. It triggered a convulsion in the party which threw the

Stevenson camp into rage and dismay and did a huge disservice to the Democratic Party. All Stevenson would say in public was: "No one can say we Democrats don't have fun." Truman, holding court in a wing chair in his hotel, was willing to bad-mouth Stevenson to all comers, including William Randolph Hearst, Jr., the heir to a newspaper chain Truman had detested. Stevenson, hearing these sad things in his hotel room, merely commented: "It does not seem to be in the interests of the party to demean one another." Truman went on breaking all bounds of sense or party discipline, as the delegates began to desert in droves from Harriman's lines. I had a private session with him, the night before the balloting, and instead of finding a mad, bad Truman, I came on a chortling bantam cock. He was delighted to talk about Stevenson. It didn't really matter who was nominated. Any moron could defeat "that General." Even you, he said, "with your accent, could do it. Now, what's on your mind?" All that was on my mind was to find out his main motive for turning on Stevenson. "Now, mind you," he began, "there's nothin' personal in this. I like the man." That, it was clear—on the Freudian principle that where the patient denies is the place to dig—was the motive: Truman had a visceral dislike of Stevenson and his American type. Quickly brushing aside the disclaimer, he ranted on about the flaws and failings of a man you might have thought was the most contemptible of the Republican hopefuls: "He's a country-club, tweedy snob, mixed up with a bunch of defeatists and reactionaries. We need a fighter like Averell Harriman. Stevenson won't listen to the pros; he just goes on with his fancy talk." This was hair-raising stuff to be peddling, on the eve of the convention, to a newspaper reporter he barely knew. It was, I can only guess, a first symptom of that softening of the conscience and hardening of the arteries which produced in his eighties a well-regulated flow of regular guy maxims, reminiscences, fictions, and obscenities masquerading as a spate of total recall. It was, at any rate, too cruel to put into print or to report back to Stevenson. When he came into his suite, after a large party at midnight, eager to know what "the old man" had said, I gave him a highly edited account, mentioning only that if he won the nomination this time, he should pay more attention to "the old pros." Contrary to the testimony of several of his advisers, Stevenson guessed at the bile in Truman's outburst and was deeply hurt by it. It took all his generosity and gentility to brace himself for a jolly appearance on the rostrum in the awful scene on the last night when Truman, Stevenson, and Kefauver—any one of whom by now, finding himself on a train, would have hastened to grab the seat farthest from the other two— had to come together and clasp their hands high like boxers or drunken dons representing the Three Graces at a college reunion. A completely unabashed Truman now hailed as "a true fighter" the softie he had done his best to strangle, and then went into this waggish passage: "Some fellah whom I shall not name has said that Governor Stevenson will have trouble winning in November. But now, let me tell you something. Don't let that worry you. That's what almost everyone else was saying about me in 1948." A cute, endearing fellow, this Truman. So I tried to stab Adlai, he was saying. Shucks, it was a rubber knife. Laugh? We thought we'd die.

What was permanently galling about this tasteless Truman performance was the grain of truth. Stevenson was by temperament as well as upbringing a conservative who happened to have been born into a family with a Democratic tradition ("a Republican for

Stevenson," Isaiah Berlin called him). He was always
more embarrassed than excited by the huge, loose
continental coalition of regional and ideological types
that make up any Democratic Party which must expect
to survive. City and rural poverty simply floored him.
Nothing in his code of noblesse oblige prepared him to
tackle it as a day-to-day political challenge. He wanted
to turn away. Moving among wretched people in mean
places, as I often saw him do, he had the humility of a
saint but not the serenity. He was acutely sensitive to
poverty, sickness, disability, and grief. But when he
was among his poorer worshipers, he could not
improvise the politician's spread-eagle stance and the
manic grin. He ambled nervously among them, spoke
gently, hoping to convey by a look that he was grateful
they did not hold their plight against him. "Grateful"
was a favorite word. When I was visited once by two
Indians who had just heard about Stevenson's plan to
make a world tour, they both jumped to the question:
would he be speaking in Bombay? I said that, as I
understood it, he was not going to speak anywhere, he
was going around to look and listen. They crumpled in
my sight, and one said, almost in furious disappoint-
ment, "If Stevenson were to speak in Bombay, a
hundred thousand untouchables would be at his feet."
When I told Stevenson about this anecdote, he blushed
very red. "You don't say?" he blurted. "I'm very
grateful."

When Stevenson returned from that world tour, he
was given a big dinner party in Chicago. Eisenhower
was once again, and even more securely, in the White
House, and the Democrats were looking around
despairingly for some new Lochinvar on the horizon.
Some of them without doubt still hankered after
Stevenson, but more looked on the Chicago banquet as
a farewell tribute, a bang-up separation allowance.

They had come to bury him, but after a thundering bit of eloquence on that last night, he found his suite swarming with Governors and old party leaders. The party had meant to write his political epitaph in the nicest way but wound up with an engraved invitation to try again. I don't believe he would ever have accepted it had Eisenhower not come down with his massive heart attack in September, 1955. In the following weeks, it was impossible not to discern a new, if tactful, gleam in Stevenson's eyes. He was duly sorry to hear that the General could not possibly run again (a distinguished surgeon's prognosis, which I passed on to Stevenson, was that "on top of the ileitis, the General'll be lucky to live another year"), but he began to yearn once more. His judgment, during the following winter, that Eisenhower's first term would be his last led to a flurry of telephone calls, visits of regional leaders, the mustering of Stevenson's demobilized army of aides and advisers, and so on to the strategy of a Stevenson with a "regular guy" face-lift, and such embarrassments as the cowboy performance in Los Banos.

What he took later to be the most tormenting of his humiliations at the hands of the Kennedy team was one in which he subsequently took some pride. This was his part in the Cuban missile crisis. Here he unhappily shared the popular misunderstanding that, as Our Man at the United Nations, he was the key American able to arrest the drift from order into chaos. The United Nations debates were exhaustively televised. Stevenson was at center stage, flailing the Soviet Union with no holds barred. He displayed alarming photographic blowups of what American military reconnaissance had discovered. This time he had been assured by the President that the photographs were all too real. So for once, Stevenson was able to indulge his most chafing rhetoric without the restraints of diplomatic nicety: "Ambassador Zorin...you are in the courtroom of world opinion. You have denied [the missiles] exist, and I want to know if I understood you correctly. I am prepared to wait for my answer until hell freezes over." Ambassador Zorin protested that he was not in the dock of an American courtroom and, hinting at the Bay of Pigs discomfiture, got in the dig that here was Mr. Stevenson with more of his pictures. Stevenson, to everybody but the White House, seemed to be the man carrying the ball. But he was not. He was the front for American indignation, making its case against the sounding board of the United Nations. By that time, the United Nations was no longer the party of the first or second part in any crisis of realpolitik. It was between the White House and the Kremlin. And the National Security Council was meeting round the clock and had already sifted through several choices when Stevenson descended on Washington to declare that what was essential was to negotiate a quid pro quo, not to assert American prestige or frighten the Russians with a show of power. He suggested that in return for a Soviet promise to withdraw the Cuban missiles, the United States should remove its missiles from Turkey. (They were not ninety miles from the Soviet Union; they were on her border. This obvious fact at once occurred to the Allied leaders in Europe, where, in the early throes of the crisis, Kennedy was feared as much as Khrushchev.) The move had already been discussed and rejected, and Stevenson felt rebuffed. He had been so busy in New York that he was not in touch with the growing complexity of the Soviet threat, from the verbal assaults of Khrushchev to the approach of Russian ships with more missiles and launching equipment. When he heard of the immense scale of American mobilization along the Florida peninsula and elsewhere, he argued testily against the men who were inclined to a direct strike against the missile bases. In the heat and tension of the Washington meetings, his unwillingness to consider any action other than the withdrawal of the Turkish missiles began to seem like a gesture of appeasement not even as creditable as Chamberlain's at Munich ("At least," said one adviser, "Britain was unarmed, and Chamberlain knew it"). Stevenson—oscillating between his own thesis and surprise at Russian moves and messages he had not heard about—appeared no better than a New York commuter offering dogmatic solutions, a telling exemplar of Machiavelli's maxim: "The absent are always wrong." He became intolerable to the military, and not only to the military. There were civilians in those meetings fairly new to the verge of war. And there was Dean Acheson, fired with the exhilaration of having had a hand in running the Second World War and Korea, and nursing an old grudge against Stevenson since the time of his first run for the presidency. (Acheson never forgot a telephone call at a time when he was being most mercilessly abused by Senator Joseph McCarthy, in which Stevenson hoped for Acheson's campaign support but awkwardly hinted that he had better not expect to be named to a Stevenson Cabinet!) These civilians—with the honorable exception of George Ball—could stand, and would stand again during the successive debacles of the Vietnam War, as warning reminders of C.E. Montague's line: "Hell hath no fury like a non-combatant scorned." They rounded on Stevenson, privately deploring his "softness" and ignorance. He was not brought into the crucial Saturday night meeting. Oddly, the one member of the National Security Council who gave Stevenson the gentlest consideration was the President himself, evidently

trying to make amends for his deception over the Bay
of Pigs. Nonetheless, Kennedy salted Stevenson's
wound by appointing John McCloy as a "special
assistant" in the negotiations at the United Nations.
McCloy was, in fact, stationed there as a watchdog
on the suspiciously "soft" Stevenson, who, in the
following weeks, saw his stand interpreted in a
magazine article as a Munich surrender, and in the
New York *Daily News* as a sure sign that "Adlai [was]
on the Skids over Pacifist Stand in Cuba."

When it was all over, the papers barely noticed that
the White House gave orders to have the Turkish
missiles dismantled—on the grounds of their ob-
solescence. Kennedy was widely praised for his
courage and firmness. Only I. F. Stone wondered
aloud what would have happened if Khrushchev had
not backed down. It is a question whose answer must
await the next nuclear bluff, which may not be between
two giants but between half a dozen nations aspiring to
giantism. As Alastair Hetherington wrote at the time:
"Life is precarious enough when the weapons of terror
lie in the hands of two men only. It will be far more
precarious when five or ten men, individually and
separately, can by misjudgment burn half the world."

THE LAST TIME I SAW STEVENSON was at a party he gave
in New York the night before he took off for a trip to
London in the summer of 1965. With all his files
attended to or shelved, he was in his most genial form,
dodging merrily between groups of thirty or forty
people of several colors and many nationalities. It was
long after midnight when they had all bowed out, and
there were only three of us left, the third party being an
old aide and a friend of over thirty years' standing. We
had yet another nightcap, and then the two of us

moved to go. As Stevenson stood at the door joshing us on our way, the friend pointed in mock horror at Stevenson's middle and patted its considerable spare tire. "I know, I know," said Stevenson, "I'm going to do something about it in Europe—they tell me." He cackled with laughter as the friend chuckled: "You know what's going to happen to you, Adlai? You'll get to London, have one more blowout and drop dead in your tracks!" We gave each other waggish digs in the ribs and slapped each other, and wished him a long and happy holiday. At two in the morning, it seemed an hilarious line.

Two days later, he dropped dead on a London street, going out in an enviable flash, as healthy men in their sixties might hope to do.

Other men had long ago replaced him in the race. He had, indeed, in 1961, been put out to pasture. But if the public Stevenson was a restless figurehead, the private man was as scrupulous and busy as ever, keeping up with scores of friends and hundreds of acquaintances, visiting the sick, telephoning condolences, dropping every week scores of notes of thanks and cheer to anonymous admirers, gravely looking over preposterous projects for a new tractor, a reformed banking system, a world government, a better mousetrap. Attending all the parties, and incidentally leaving four or five women I can think of with the secret conviction that they were the one, and that if they played their cards properly, they could have something there—including, certainly, marriage.

What he left behind was something more splendid, in a public man, than a record of power. It was simply an impression—of goodness. He had mastered the art, far more difficult and rarer than that of a successful politician, writer, musician, actor: success as a human being. Was he, then, too good to be a politician? Yes, in the sense of being too touchy to weather feuds and grievances, too gentle to take the rough-and-tumble. This courtly, twinkling, roly-poly comical man was of that estimable order of Americans—Henry Clay, Robert E. Lee, Norman Thomas, Learned Hand, perhaps Wendell Willkie—who left a lasting impression by the energy of their idealism but who were never quite strong or ruthless enough, in the pit of the political jungle and the critical relations of life, to turn goodness and mercy into law or policy. Maybe it can never be done. At any rate, Adlai Stevenson remains the liveliest reminder of our time that there are admirable reasons for failing to be President.

V

BERTRAND RUSSELL

The Lord of Reason

IT WAS NOT YET SEVEN in the morning on a Sunday in winter, and there were very few people about in the concourse of Pennsylvania Station. We had arranged to meet at the newsstand rather than the Washington track because he liked to mooch around the book displays, and he approved of American railroad station architecture, which allows the traveler to wander around in a cathedral of light and warmth before descending to the dark cave where the trains leave from. It dawns on only the very old in England that waiting for a train on the same level as a concourse which is open to the winter winds is an unnecessary discomfort, no matter how adorably the station is festooned with Victorian ironwork.

In those days—it was 1950—Pennsylvania Station had not yet been torn apart and converted into airport arcade modern. It was a raw morning, and I was glad of our arrangement as I entered the Tepidarium of the

Baths of Caracalla, of which the Pennsylvania concourse was a splendid copy.

The newsstand was not yet open, but he was there just the same, pattering up and down and stopping from time to time to peer in at the riches he couldn't get his hands on, like a caged animal impatient for feeding time.

From even a short distance he could fairly have been mistaken for a beggar. A very small man in a green topcoat that was too big for him (was it his?) and was green not from chic but from age. He held a pipe to his mouth, and he walked with that deliberate flexing motion of the legs which old people have to use to walk evenly, or choose to use to show they are sprightlier than people thought. If he had ever appeared in Beverly Hills like that, with his frayed coat and slouchy hat, he would have been arrested on the spot. And even in New York I doubt he could have gone on pattering and peering for long without some cop strolling over to him. I imagined a Frank Capra vignette, in which the cop was affable but on the ball, and saying, "Pardon me, you got a home? Going someplace, brother?" And the old beggar replying with snapping precision: "I am Bertrand Arthur William, third Earl Russell, at present residing at Richmond, Surrey, and shortly on my way to Stockholm, Sweden, to receive the Nobel Prize for Literature. In the meantime, I am going to Washington to see my daughter Kate."

It is a charming scene to dwell on, but Russell, not being Noel Coward or even Monty Woolley, would never have come through with such a snappy riposte. He didn't disdain his title, but when it came to him, in his sixtieth year, on the death of his brother, he thought of it as "a great nuisance" which could, however, be got rid of only if he was "attainted of high treason, a method [that] seems to me perhaps somewhat extreme." Twenty years later, several peers renounced their title on its inheritance without having their heads cut off on Tower Hill. But Russell was never prepared to make a spectacle of renunciation. He simply put out a public statement that he would use the title only on formal occasions and instructed his publishers not to use it "in connection with any of my literary work." If you probed him about it, he was quite clear about why he put up with the "great nuisance." It was part of his heritage. It did not affect either his character or his social views, and—the only time it came up—I had the feeling that he had nothing but contempt for men who, in spurning their father's title, adopted a mucker's pose to make a show of their common humanity. Throughout all his battles against privilege, tyranny, poverty, party politics, and the rest, he did not deplore the Establishment as such but only an Establishment that had lapsed from its duties and obligations. His lifelong attitude toward the root problem of a classless society was stated once for all when the First World War exposed him—not least as a pacifist in prison—to the world of ordinary people: "When I examine my own conception of human excellence, I find that, doubtless owing to early environment, it contains many elements which have hitherto been associated with aristocracy, such as fearlessness, independence of judgment, emancipation from the herd, and leisurely culture. Is it possible to preserve these qualities, and even make them widespread, in an industrial community? And is it possible to dissociate them from the typical aristocratic vices: limitation of sympathy, haughtiness, and cruelty to those outside a charmed circle?"

Everything of the sort that he had written—his abundant and never-ending pleas for tolerance, compassion, kindness, love of one's fellowman—

prepared one for a gentle creature, almost timorous in expressing any opinion, as good people so often are. And it was heartening to see how, with his children and grandchildren, he was full of domestic solicitude, accepted almost with relief the most modest cottage life, and with small children especially rollicked in their rebelliousness and artless play. But in adult society he was a forbidding man. He was back on enemy territory, where other men's prejudices, greed, slipshod thoughts, and unpleasant opinions had to be fought and routed. Out in the world, whether he was lecturing, arguing, or expounding his current mission, he was not a man for small talk or friendly kidding. At a lunch in Washington that preceded a television appearance, the hosts obviously expected the old soldier to be in mufti, but he was driven to fury, and threatened to leave the table, when he was baited for his Socialist views by a woman journalist hot for domestic Communists but indifferent, as he told her, to the means of hunting them.

I KNEW ALL THIS WELL ENOUGH when I walked into Pennsylvania Station. I had listened to him often in public. But this time the auspices were well calculated to make me revise my view of him and take him at his face value as a venerable sage. He was in America on a lecture tour, and one day his agent telephoned me and said he would be happy if I could go and call on him. It was a summons to the Pope, and I arrived, fairly nervous, at the New York apartment he was staying in. When I knocked on the door, it was opened by a large woman, rose-faced—and bosomed, I imagined—who clapped her hands as at the return of the prodigal. Russell rose from an armchair and said, "Ah!" It was an eloquent welcome, from a man who, however articulate, did not waste words. He wasted no time, either, on genteel preliminaries but announced, like a headmaster awarding the annual English prize: "I asked you here, Cooke, because I wanted to tell you that whenever I read your pieces in the *Guardian*, I say to myself: That is probably the way it happened." There, he seemed to say, what do you think of that? What did I *think*? I was delirious, foolish with pride. I said I thought it was very handsome indeed, and whenever I wasn't sure myself about "the way it happened," I'd take his word for it. "Splendid, splendid," he intoned in his high nasal voice, and waved his pipe in the air. It was a compliment all the more acceptable at the time, because I had for the better part of a year been sweating at the trials of Alger Hiss, and had just put out a book about them, and I didn't know then for sure "the way it happened," and still don't.

At any rate, the reader will be forewarned by this bout of flattery and appreciate why, when he called and asked me if I should like to go with him to Washington, I canceled everything on the calendar, including my Sunday piece for the paper (which was always expected to be, as Sir Walter Scott put it, "the Big Bow-Wow") and set the alarm for five forty-five, something I have not done since.

GREETING ME AT THE CLOSED NEWSSTAND, he gave me a perfunctory smile and, pointing his pipe at the shutters, snapped, "If they run trains as early as this, why can't they have the bookstall open?" I had no theory about this dereliction, so we walked up and down while he humphed and puffed his pipe. Pretty soon, though, a shutter went rattling up, and behind it a fat man in a sweater was seen snipping the ropes off shoulder-high bundles of *The New York Times* and pausing from time to time to blow on his coffee in a cardboard cup. "Come along, man!" Russell was muttering, but the man looked at us from his fishbowl and took long slurping drafts of his coffee. Russell was surprisingly put out by this languid proletarian, who had the aristocratic virtues of "fearlessness, independence of judgment, emancipation from the herd," as well as the aristocratic vices of "limitation of sympathy, haughtiness, and cruelty to those outside a charmed circle." Eventually, he opened up the stand and, I shall not easily forget, leaned affably on a stack of magazines and said, "Now, granddad, what's on your mind?" Russell ignored the newspapers and magazines and looked wonderingly over row upon row of paperback thrillers, best sellers, science fiction, movie-star confessionals, and the usual reprints of classics got up with three-color jackets suggesting sexual hanky-panky undiscovered by the English Lit. major. Russell promptly pointed to three or four whodunits, bought and pocketed them, and said, "How marvelous to have all this on tap. One of the most beastly things about austerity in England is that we simply won't release the paper to print enough paperback books."

We went off to the train in much better spirits, settled in two dumpy elbow chairs of the parlor car, and were soon sliding under the river and out onto the Wellsian industrial nightmare of the Jersey flats. "I remember all this," said Russell, "before we reaped the benefits of the Industrial Revolution. It was all countryside, except for little manufacturing towns made of brick." He guessed—with what seemed at the time to be lurid pessimism—at the coming blight of the cities, and that led on to a rising crime rate and other such routine lamentations.

I kept detailed notes of this trip, but if I now had a

tape recording of the train ride to Washington, I'm sure the striking feature of it would be the almost sentientious precision of Russell's talk, generations away from the trailing sentences, the staggering caesuras, the chattering overlap dialogue which the most modish of modern film directors try to convince us is the true style of human conversation. When Russell was angry—which was very often if a moral principle or a political squabble was concerned—he delivered himself of a perfectly composed operatic aria, albeit with the tone of a bagpipe. But also when he was at his most meditative and agreeable, as he was now, he still composed everything in his head and pronounced it with medodious, if nasal, finality. The nasal quality was almost telephonic, and my tapes—if they had ever been made—would sound like examples of a Dial-an-Aphorism service.

Gun control was not then an issue. But as the petticoats of an old manufacturing town drifted by, and a worn sign said "Glassworks," Russell brightened and went into a startling story which I frankly disbelieved—or thought of as a truth outrageously embroidered—until I read it, in persuasive detail, in his autobiography. "My first wife's cousin," he said, "was the manager of a glassworks, here in New Jersey. And he had a wife who carried a revolver till the day she died." I thought he had brought this up as the one-case, eighteen-carat proof that Americans were always a violent lot. But his face creased into a foxy grin as he ended the story with a bang: "She had absurd literary ambitions and wrote very bad plays, which nobody would put on. Consequently, she collected her husband's love letters, which she had preserved, and stuck them in her blouse and shot herself through the heart—first, of course, through the love letters."

This was the kind of anecdote, I was to discover,

that by its violent neatness put him in a good humor. In a political discussion, he would blow hot and witheringly cold, and when he had made his point, he would relapse into a kind of smoldering satisfaction. But what delighted him was the memory of a meeting, a famous anecdote, a short, sharp melodrama that ended, or could be made to end, with a maxim or a shocking punch line. It may explain his rabid appetite for whodunits. They satisfied his lifetime's search for an order he could not find in human affairs, and they tickled the love of violence which lies not far beneath the surface of the intellectual who protests at all times his passion for reason. ("Life," he once wrote, "is nothing but a competition to be the criminal rather than the victim.")

The mention of the small New Jersey town—it was Millville—where he had first stayed in America took him back to other memories of his first visit, in 1896, when he was only twenty-four. On a Sunday in New York he had watched his first parade. Easter? "It may well have been Easter, although the society folk made a point of parading in their finery on Fifth Avenue on any Sunday when the weather was pleasant. But on that occasion, I remember the crowds somewhere in the Fifties, all very excited and crowding round a particular street corner. I thought there'd been an accident. The people were craning their necks and shouting, 'Where is it? Have you seen it?'" What was it all about? He would lean back before any punch line with his neck rigid and his pipe held out before the final pronouncement. "Well, all the fuss was about a French invention that had appeared on the streets for the first time. I believe, later on, the Americans did something about it. It was called *l'automobile*."

The terrors of what "the Americans did" to the automobile led him on to his present obsession, which was with the effect of science—of the nuclear age more than anything—on government and the balance of power. The train was no place to start a seminar, and he knew that I had heard his lectures on the topic, given the previous week at Columbia University. But as we went in to breakfast, he said what a pleasure it had been to see the theater packed with so many attentive young people. They constituted, he remarked with a faint smile, "a very acceptable revenge on their elders." I had not wanted to broach what had been probably the most painful of all his American experiences. But in the evident joy of a tremendous reception in New York, he was more than willing to talk about the kindness and "belated" sympathy he had had from the academics who had attended the Columbia lectures, and to mark with acidulous asides the contrast with his ordeal of ten years before, which had offered an inglorious demonstration of the New York City Establishment in one of its periodic spasms of civic indignation. In February, 1940, wearying of what he had come to feel was the "almost totalitarian atmosphere" of the University of California under President Robert Sproul, Russell snapped up the invitation of a professorship at the College of the City of New York. He was to teach the theory of logic, but he had probably forgotten that to an old enemy, William Thomas Manning, Bishop of the Protestant Episcopal Diocese of New York, Bertrand Russell in any academic guise was "a recognized propagandist against religion and morality" and "a defender of adultery." The Jesuits took up the warning cry against "a desiccated, divorced, and decadent advocate of sexual promiscuity." They were followed by a scandalized housewife, who brought a case in the State Supreme Court to order the college to rescind Russell's appointment. The presiding judge was a Roman

Catholic who had once urged the removal of a likeness of Martin Luther from a courthouse mural (illustrating a history of law, not religion). The judge obliged, citing Russell's legal status as an alien (a refugee from the European war when the United States was determined not to get into it), adding Russell's lamentable failure "to have passed a competitive examination," adding also the gratuitous judicial opinion that in honoring its contract, the college would be "in effect establishing a chair of indecency." Mayor La Guardia short-circuited an appeal by briskly canceling the appropriation for Russell's salary. Russell had at his back a small army of disgusted academes and journalists, but ahead of him he had the prospect of an income of no more than $1000 in the coming year. He had a wife to keep and two children at the University of California, and nothing else coming in. His gloom was exacerbated by the appalling news from Europe: Hitler had invaded the Low Countries and was on his way to Dunkirk. Russell longed to be in England, wondered in a letter to Lord Halifax, the British Ambassador, if he ought to go back (Halifax, in a masterpiece of diplomatic fuzz, replied, "It all depends"), and wrote sorrowfully to a friend: "My personal ruin passes unnoticed. So I am apt to feel cross, and as I mustn't let it out on my enemies, I snap at my friends."

This visit, on the contrary, had been a triumph. His tour had started with a philosophy course at Mount Holyoke, and while he was giving it, he was invited to do three lectures at Columbia University. Between Holyoke and Columbia, the news came in that he had won the Nobel Prize for Literature. He appeared on three successive days at twilight, and if he had had the faintest interest in publicity or promotion, he would have anticipated the mobs of merely curious citizens who would come to gape at the latest international

184

celebrity. But there was also a solid pack of students there who had heard, or just read, about his old ordeal with City College, and when the bony little figure with the thatch of white hair appeared from the wings, the theater trembled with the stamping feet and baying applause of the young who were exulting in the victory of an undefeatable seventy-eight-year-old.

After breakfast on the train, he remarked that "the City College commotion was, in the long view, only the culmination of a lifetime's battle with bigots in authority. Much the same thing happened, on a more modest scale, on my very first visit. I was brought here, don't you know, by my first wife."

"To New Jersey?"

"More accurately, to Bryn Mawr."

His wife, Alys Pearsall Smith, was of a rich Philadelphia Quaker family and had recently graduated from Bryn Mawr. She was evidently eager to show the bridegroom off, possibly as a coming young English brain, no doubt also as the son of Lord Amberley.

"I contrived to give some lectures on the foundations of geometry, which attracted what I then thought of as an enormous audience, thirty students at least. But none of the elite of American mathematicians had ever heard of me, and one of them assured the president of the college that I was a dilettante. However, the president was a cousin of my wife's, a Dr. Carey Thomas, a dragon of virtue, the Bishop Manning, you might say, of Bryn Mawr. If she thought I was a dilettante, she was to encounter much worse in her cousin. Alys had three preoccupations at the time: the suffrage movement, the temperance movement, and free love. She undertook to lecture in and about Bryn Mawr on the first two. But her enthusiasm for the third—which I am glad to say was quite theoretical at the time—well, it got the better of her. It was altogether too much for the formidable Dr. Thomas, and we soon left Bryn Mawr under a cloud."

Russell chuckled with great relish over this early brush with the puritans and made a final point after a long draw on his pipe: "Many years later, I was invited to lecture at Bryn Mawr again. Dr. Thomas was still the president, but by that time Alys and I had parted, which only confirmed her first low opinion of me. She absolutely forbade me to appear before the student body. It was always a very comely student body, and she feared for their chastity. She was probably," he ended with a grin, "quite right. Dr. Thomas, I must say though, was a Tartar." (The Tartar was later to be immortalized, not uncharitably, in a painstaking biography written by a Bryn Mawr teacher, one Edith Finch, who was to become Russell's fourth, last, and only satisfactory wife, in his eightieth year.)

"Well," he said, as if to put an end to all this amusing trivia, and reached into his topcoat pocket for the three or four paperback thrillers. It was my cue to quiz him no more. He began to flick the pages over, and at first I thought he was in the habit of skipping through such frivolous stuff. But I noticed that his head went up and down in a slight but steady rhythm, and his right hand turned the pages in rapid sequence. He was a page reader. It could not have been more than fifteen minutes later that he dropped the first book on the floor and started on a second one. Another fifteen minutes, and he had finished that one. He looked up with a benevolent smile, as if he had taken a prescribed pill—two pills—and began again to reminisce, as the station stops were called off or as stretches of remembered landscape inspired him.

I don't remember—or didn't note down—any other American memories, but at some point he began to philosophize about his long link with the two countries and some of their eminent dead. Not exactly to philosophize but to riffle through a sketchbook of his contemporaries, the more unpleasant the better to damn in a caption. As everybody has noticed about the old, their memory seems to grow sharper about the long-gone years as it grows dimmer about the immediate past. The effect on the listener, as they recall childhood memories, is to turn the past into the historic present. And soon Russell was talking about people fifty years apart as if they were all characters in the cast of a play that was not yet over. I egged him on in this fascinating exercise by mentioning that once, in the early thirties in Wyoming, I had met an old man who knew Frémont, the American explorer who, among other innovations, opened up the northern route beyond the Mississippi into Wyoming. I said something to the effect that looking at that old man, I had the eerie feeling of being in touch with what now seems like America's Middle Ages.

He was not, I think, greatly impressed by this imagined association with a man who, after all, had not died until 1890. But it tickled his vanity sufficiently to make him say, "A little later on, you'll find that that old man will be more vivid than President Truman." I started to toss at him the names of the heroes and ogres of my boyhood, and he responded in just the way I'd hoped, though whether it was my unfortunate choice of names or the expression of a waspish mood, they all came out ogres. H. G. Wells: "A vain man, with a good fund of original ideas, who was spoiled by his ambition to be thought upper-middle class. I remember a disastrous visit he once paid me with his wife. Although he himself had a marked Cockney accent, he kept upbraiding his wife for possessing one." Bernard Shaw he dismissed with a single savage blow: "He wanted to be witty at all costs and it led him into unbelievable cruelties. He taunted Wells with facetious remarks about his wife—Wells's wife—when he knew very well she was dying of cancer."

We were now well along the path of retracing his earliest contemporaries, and they might have been present-day idols he found unimpressive. Tennyson? "Tennyson was an appalling exhibitionist. He thought of himself as a combination of Homer and Sir Henry Irving. He used to go swaggering along country lanes reciting aloud and swinging a cloak. He had an almost theatrically pink complexion and two red spots on his cheeks. I think he used makeup." Had he known Browning? "Oh, dear, yes. A frightful bore. He used to come round to the house to read his poems to the ladies at teatime. A bouncy man. A showoff, too. Really a Helen Hokinson cartoon character."

We turned to politics, and recalling his *Practice and Theory of Bolshevism*—in the wake of which he was, typically, embraced by his conservative enemies and denounced by his Socialist friends—I asked him if he had ever met Lenin. Lenin was to a few of my own contemporaries in the 1920s a demigod, but to many more Mephistopheles reincarnated. To everybody I knew he was a leader as exotic and sinister as Genghis Khan, and it would have been impossible to imagine his ever being buried, as comfortable, dandruffy old Marx was, in Highgate. Russell replied very deliberately: "I think he was the most evil man—and certainly one of the most imperturbable—I ever met. He had steady black eyes that never flickered. I hoped to make them flicker at one point by asking him why it was thought necessary to murder hundreds of thousands of kulaks. He quite calmly ignored the word 'murder.' He smiled and said they were a nuisance that stood in the way of his agricultural plans." I mumbled the unoriginal thought that Lenin must have been a terrifying man to sit opposite.

"Perhaps. But not to me. I had been inoculated in boyhood against such men"—a long, wheezing draw on the pipe—"by my first encounter with Mr. Gladstone. Gladstone came to our house to dinner when I was, I suppose, no more than sixteen or seventeen. There was no other man in the house. The dinner, I imagine, went off well enough, for he was surrounded by my female relations, most of them Whigs with the liveliest interest in prisons and social reform and so on. But when they retired, I was left alone with Gladstone. He made no effort to put me at my ease. He sat there saying nothing, with his ferocious face and his basilisk eye, which he turned on me— reprovingly—from time to time. I was petrified with fright. Then I appreciated that I was failing in my duty as a host. I stretched my foot under the table to find the bell, and in due course the butler appeared. I ordered the port. There was another dreadful silence. At last it came. He looked at it suspiciously for what seemed an age, and then he took a sip. At last, he said, 'Capital port you have here. How *odd* that you serve it in a claret glass.' After that, Lenin had no terrors for me."

If he could go back to Gladstone, why not to "Our Gracious Queen" herself? No problem. Since she had lived nearly thirty years after his birth, of course he had met her. But now, well launched on this return voyage, he preferred to recall—or affect to recall—his first memory of her, when he sat on her lap during a tea party at his grandparents' house, Pembroke Lodge: "A tea cozy, I think, would describe her adequately." He was two years old at the time. In case I suspected that this was what Mark Twain called "a stretcher," he quickly recalled "a much more memorable trauma, perhaps a year or so later, though I was later told it happened when I fell out of my mother's carriage. I fell down one day and bruised my penis. Like every other boy at the time, I was supposed not to notice that I had one. Nevertheless, my nurse was instructed to teach me how to sponge it in a hot bath."

His father had died when he was three, and his mother and sister—of the then mortal diphtheria— when he was one and a half. But the mention of his grandparents set him off on the vast social changes since the vanished age they had lived in. If Russell's own life was to span, as Ronald Clark puts it, "General Grant's presidency and Nixon's reign," the grandparents who helped to bring him up had spanned the reign of Robespierre and Grant's second term. He had the warmest memories of his grandfather, Lord John Russell, Prime Minister, Foreign Secretary, the great Whig champion of Parliamentary reform, who had died when Russell was six. But Russell must have tired long ago of talking about the political grandeurs and miseries of the famous man. On this train ride, it was clear, he was much more interested in the private whimsies of the great. Somehow his grandfather's support of the Duke of Wellington's Ministry came up, and after that the name of Napoleon. Without a trace of self-consciousness, Russell made a wry face and said, "A thoroughly nasty man, I was told. I had an aunt who went once or twice to Versailles and danced with him. She took a dim view of him: he danced, she said, on his stummick!"

On this astonishing note, Russell hunched his shoulders and sank into his chair, saying: "Napoleon, as you may know, had an automatic inner clock. He could sleep anywhere, at any time, for just as long or as little as he chose. I shall do the same."

He folded his hands across his lap, the long bony fingers and the patches of liver spots running up to his wrists. The asperity faded from his features. He slumped further down, so it seemed that his angular small head would soon disappear into a collar at least three sizes too big for him. He had been called by many images in his time: a snapping pike, an odd fish, a rare bird, an angry eagle, and—by ex-wives—a goblin and a demon. Shrunken now, as old people are, in a suit that flapped around his bones, he was a sleepy eaglet nestling into its father's clothes. He was asleep almost at once.

I looked at him and thought how absurdly wide is the range of human tolerance of pain and misfortune. The sight of a cockroach can produce hysteria in A; an unpaid bill, ulcers in B; a life sentence on innocent C induces stoicism or perpetual grumbling about a leaky faucet. W. S. Gilbert, a misanthrope if ever there was one, wrote in a bitter mood a quatrain that would have anthology status, along with Eliot and Frost, if it had been set to music by Mozart or Verdi: "See how the Fates their gifts allot,/ For A is happy, B is not./ Yet B is worthy, I dare say,/ Of more prosperity than A." Here was a man whose life was, by his own egotistical effort, an open book: an act of narcissism that bared him to every sort of enemy and guaranteed he would have ninety-eight years of a fitful fever. Yet it was not possible, it was not possible for me certainly, to look back on it without enormous, if qualified, admiration. It could be said that the First Act of his life, up to the First World War, was the predictable ferment of a gifted and neurotic Cambridge intellectual who chose to throw himself into academic controversy, political protest, Fabian causes, and a sequence of love affairs sparked by simple lust but rationalized, and agonized over, as experiments in human freedom. After that, though, came the Second Act heralded by the Guns of August. He was forty-two years old and geared for sterner troubles. He was, he announced, prepared "to play Faust, for whom Mephistopheles was represented by the Great War." Between the beginning of it and the end of the Second War, he withstood imprisonment, debt, the alienation of friends, D. H. Lawrence, Soviet Communism, a nearly mortal illness, fatherhood (at fifty-nine), the shattering and remaking of his fundamental beliefs, the wrath of two American universities, the repudiation and then the favor of the British Foreign Office, an unrelentingly vicious campaign of slander by the American academic and newspaper Establishment, near poverty, "despair beyond bearing," and the ecstasy and exhaustion of five grand passions (neatly entombed in the index of his autobiography under "Russell, Bertrand Arthur William—Loves").

Throughout these thirty years, he never relaxed to cultivate his garden (in a literal sense, gardens were among his greatest pleasures). He refused, even in the throes of the most baffling mathematical problems, to let the world go by. Early in the First War, the success of the Germans before the Battle of the Marne provoked him to a public protest against "the massacre of the young of any nationality," and he threw in an extra bit of spleen against "the men of Westminster who are tortured by patriotism." Understandably, he was a powerful nuisance, and went to jail. When the war was over, he was eager to see the next new social order and went off to Russia well disposed to believe in the courage and effectiveness of the great experiment, but he was outraged by the "cruelty, poverty, suspicion, persecution that formed the very air we breathed," an air admiringly breathed, nonetheless, by his accompanying friends. Then he decided to tackle "the hypocrisy and incompetence of our educational system" and nearly bankrupted himself by founding and running a school on principles of "training, initiative, discouraging prudery and restraints on freedom," but the whooping progressives who were just then enthralled by such things balked at his equally firm insistence on "scholastic instruction and a code of discipline," and—help!—"the absence of the opportunity for exciting pleasures." Down all these years, he keeps telling himself, and publishing tracts to make a religion of it, that marriage achieves dignity only by the freedom of the partners to cherish other intimate relationships. But when his girl sleeps with another man, he is racked with jealousy and "a sense of the sanctuary defiled."

HE WOKE UP as the train lurched into the Washington station. His watery eyes were clear again, and he had that amused benign look that the old—and babies—take on after the shortest rest. He left the two read thrillers on the floor, pocketed the other two, and we went off to the kind of public chore he had borne all his life: the interview, the lunch of admirers and skeptics, the television show (it was, I think, *Meet the Press*), then another interview, and so on to his daughter's house.

He came over the next year for the opening night of the annual forum of the New York *Herald Tribune*, to whose mainly Republican audience—he presumed—he was careful to introduce himself as a Socialist supporter of the British Labor government who cared more about individual liberty than any other thing and that on that ground, above all others, he opposed Communism and always had. He was in a dinner jacket. "Moscow," he said, "is fond of referring to me as a wolf in a dinner jacket. I seldom wear one, but I want you to know that so far as tonight is concerned, the Moscow statement is a half-truth." It was the only glimmer of humor. He spoke on "New Hopes for a Changing World" before an audience that was polite but not deeply excited by his familiar message that "the application of science to industry, by revolutionizing man's relation to nature, has destroyed the old equilibrium that existed in man's relation to other men and to himself... the world is facing a prospective disaster and is asking itself in a bewildered way why there seems to be no escape from a tragic fate that no one desires." It ended with a modest proposal delivered in a soothing and reasonable cadence so strikingly at variance with the snappish tone in which Russell conducted private political discussions: equality must be substituted for love of domination, justice for love of victory, intelligence for brutality; and since "happiness and the means to happiness depend upon harmony with other men," people had only "to think and feel in this way" and they would find that "not only their personal problems, but all the problems of world politics, even the most abstruse and difficult, would melt away... and the beauty of the world would take possession."

There was not much to take hold of here during a year which had witnessed, among other expressions of harmony among men, the sentencing of Ilse Koch for obscene brutalities at Buchenwald; the rise to power of Senator Joseph McCarthy through his characterization of General George Marshall as a traitor and an assassin; the exposure by Senator Estes Kefauver of a national crime syndicate buying protection from businessmen and politicians; the American suspension of all tariff concessions to the Soviet Union and Communist China; Britain's mulish refusal to join six other nations of Western Europe in a European Coal and Steel Plan, and a paroxysm of disunity between

Washington, the United Nations in New York, and the UN Allies in Korea which decided President Truman to strip General Douglas MacArthur of his Far Eastern command.

Whenever it was possible to confront Russell in private with the real world and gingerly inquire about the solutions he had in mind to such knotty conflicts as I have listed, he would deliver a series of judgments: Truman was quite right to fire MacArthur; Britain was wrong to stay out of the European plan; the links between crime, business, and politics only went to show that Socialism was right and necessary. Otherwise, he retreated with energetic dogmatism into the verities and shucked off any personal civic responsibility by repeating in informal variations the confession that opens his autobiography: "Three passions, simple but overwhelmingly strong, have governed my life: the longing for love, the search for knowledge, and unbearable pity for the suffering of mankind."

This splendid credo often reminded me of George Bernard Shaw's equally heroic encyclical: "This is the true joy in life, the being used for a purpose recognized by yourself as a mighty one; the being thoroughly worn out before you are thrown on the scrap heap; the being a force of Nature instead of a feverish selfish little clod of ailments and grievances complaining that the world will not devote itself to making you happy. And also the only real tragedy in life is the being used by personally minded men for purposes which you recognize to be base." This sort of thing gives one to wonder for what mighty purpose a ticket collector or a coal miner imagines himself to be used, or with how much joy a postal clerk or a janitor is free to choose between the patronage of a personally minded man or that of a state-minded commissar. Similarly, Russell's

habitual and cavalier retreats into moral injunctions
always made me uneasy at the thought of his drafting a
farm bill, setting up a nuclear inspection system,
adjudicating a case of fraud, or a neighbors' quarrel
over property rights, or any other of the great and
humble issues that politicians and lawyers have to deal
with before "the problems of world politics, even the
most abstruse and difficult, would melt away...and
the beauty of the world would take possession."

It was with this disturbing trait in mind that I seized
the chance, four years later, to hear him address an
election rally. I had been brought over to Britain by my
editor to try my hand at covering a British election, and
I wandered around the country for the whole length of
the campaign—all of ten days!—watching the British
electoral antics which, compared with the American,
are as a prayer meeting to a Roman circus. I heard that
Russell was going to appear in Glasgow in support of a
Labor candidate who had lost last time, by only a few
hundred votes, in a fairly seedy suburb. The issues, as
the opposing election agents filled me in on them, had
to do with a controversial act of Parliament
about subsidies to faltering industries, with the rising
retail price index, with the benefits to the community—
if any—of the local Cooperative Society. It would be
instructive, I thought, to watch Russell come down
from his empyrean to tackle what the Scottish oldsters
called brass tacks and the youngsters were learning to
call the nitty-gritty.

Twelve or thirteen hundred people had gathered in
the Rio Cinema, an impressive crowd for a Sunday
night sermon, almost as many as would jam the place
for *The Ring of Fear*, a Mickey Spillane horror offered
on weeknights. They sat remarkably still, turning on
coughers, very conscious of having an old wise man
come bearing hopeful oracles. He appeared even tinier

than usual against the huge CinemaScope screen, and as the respectful applause flowed in on him, he snapped his eaglet eyelids and flexed his arms at the elbows in a "hey, presto" motion, like a charming puppet.

In case any there were unsure who he was—and it is very likely that there were plenty—he would introduce himself. He was Bertrand Russell, a Liberal when most of them were in their perambulators. He had stayed with the Liberals until he discovered "in the First World War that under the guise of seeking peace they had surreptitiously committed the country to war." So for the forty succeeding years he had supported wholeheartedly the Socialist cause. Now, how about the retail price index, the subsidies, and the glories of the Rutherglen Co-op?

Of course, his thoughts on these local matters were not to be expected. He soared off at once into lofty regions where the audience might peer at him but couldn't follow him. He had come there, all the way up from London, to press on them, "and on the notice of the country the need for a world authority which will put an end to war, for in the opinion of the best men of science it is quite likely that a great war employing hydrogen bombs would put an end to the human race.... We should not have the sort of world the Russians want, nor the sort of world the Americans want, and you would certainly not get the sort of world that any of *us* want." By now, the atom bomb was "a nice friendly weapon like the bow and arrow." It was no use "declaring the hydrogen bomb to be an abomination and then trying to forget it." If war broke out tomorrow, it would be made and very likely used. And that was not the end: "There is nothing final about the dreadful ingenuities of science. There will be chemical and bacteriological warfare, and after that satellites that circle the earth and bomb the enemy every time they pass that way."

What could be done about it? He would tell them. First, we must accept limitations on national sovereignty and call a world conference in which "the casting voice lay with the neutrals" (with Chile, Albania, Uganda, South Africa, Communist China?). The nations must disarm. The United Nations must be reformed. Poverty, "which is wholly unnecessary," would have to go.

It may be callous to say that he went on and on in this way, without ever hinting how "the nations" could be made to disarm, how the United Nations could be reformed in a workable way, why "the neutrals" would be necessarily disinterested judges, how the arrested protagonists could be bullied into loving each other. At each announcement of the vague, shining alternative to war, the stolid housekeepers pounded their hands in the hope that belief would create its object. He ended, as always, clenching his bony hands to grasp the vision that eludes us all and begged them to go away and "bring about" an era "of happiness such as has never existed before...a kind of kindliness, of friendliness between men and men.... If we would, we could make life splendid and beautiful."

The decent crowd clapped him all the way out on his careful legs. When he had gone, the lucky Mr. McAllister, the Labor candidate he had backed, was in the uncomfortable spot of following a sermon on the Resurrection with a vestryman's search for the boy who had broken the parsonage window. (It was his Conservative opponent, "or his bosses." We were down to the nitty-gritty in no time.) Mr. McAllister, by the way, lost by seven times the size of his previous defeat.

I caught Russell before he was off to his night train. He was, admittedly, eighty-three and four years older than when I had last seen him. But he looked like some gnome from another planet, gray and bloodless. As we walked out of the building to a car that was waiting for him, he talked with little animation about the possible outcome of the election, which was between a prospective Clement Attlee and an Anthony Eden administration. (Eden won.) Just before I left him, I asked him flatly what he thought of Eden. He glared at me and pulled the name out of his memory and looked at it. He shook his head in a quick irritable motion. "Not a gentleman," he said, "dresses too well." The old man still had blood in him.

My report, headlined "Lord Russell's Apocalypse," appeared in the next morning's *Guardian*. It was, at more satirical length, much as I have written it here. I heard later that he had seen it and "disapproved" of it. The "kind of kindliness, of friendliness between men and men," that was going to make life "splendid and beautiful" was not quite ready to come my way. I never heard from him again. And saw him once only, bareheaded in Trafalgar Square, shouting into a bitter east wind some rasping plea to ban the bomb, or beware of the Americans, or denounce the Russians for going into Hungary. He grew increasingly frail, but he was never senile, and he went tottering down the black decade of the 1960s slapping at any injustice, however small, embracing any cause, however unpopular. You would imagine him finally exhausted, being fed gruel in his stuffy library, but suddenly he would be in the papers and on the barricades, again urging a preventive nuclear strike against the Russians, then denying he'd ever said it, then taking up the cudgels for Eugene McCarthy or Mao Tse-tung or Daniel Cohn-Bendit, or the New Left or the Pill. And nobody ever mentioned his complaining about his arthritic hands or rickety legs, for not the least of his aristocratic virtues was a disdain for seeming, in Shaw's phrase, to be "a little clod of ailments and grievances complaining that the world would not devote itself to making you happy."

THERE IS ONE SIDE OF HIM I have not touched on, and it is not from tact or primness. His "need of women" was abiding until God knows what age, and he was the first to admit it. ("Chastity: I gave it a good try once, but never again.") Either the first or second time I met him, he told me with unashamed glee about a time when he was very ill—I can't remember now whether it was the time in China he was given up for dead or, more likely, the time his plane crashed on a flight from Oslo to Trondheim, when, in his seventies, he swam in a perishing sea to safety. He woke up in a hospital, and when the clincial crisis was over, and he was comfortable, a nurse came to him whom he found "motherly but sexually attractive." Under her nurse's jacket there was apparently nothing but the nurse. Russell was happy to notice this, and with a foxy grin he implied what an absolute respect for the truth would require me to infer never happened. During his wartime stay in Princeton, when he was in his early seventies, the groves of academe were flustered by rumors of Lord Russell's goatish ways. One lady whose testimony is to be trusted made the shivering confession that the groping of the noble lord in an automobile conveyed the sensation of "dry leaves rustling up your thighs."

I find this not at all culpable and put it down here because Russell himself would have frankly admitted it. But he might in a mellow moment also have admitted that lechery was a curse and got men into situations that came to entail impossible involvements. When he first went to Paris, he was appalled and disgusted by what he saw around him as the sordid truckling to male sexuality. He was enough of a puritan and a very conscious intellectual to have to explain to himself every sexual call of nature as a fated invitation to a mystical union of souls, an incurable form of rationalization that got him into perpetual trouble. Toward the end of his life, thrashing away at the problem of sex as relentlessly as at every other problem, he put out a papal bull on the subject. Marriage was an unlivable institution because it demanded "intolerable intimacy." He implied not so much the wear and tear of different, or competing, personalities as the growing offensiveness of knowing everything about the partner's aches and pains and physical fusses and bathroom habits. Every married person has thought of this sometime or other, but in agonizing over it, Russell seems to me to be expressing the morbid sensitiveness of the uncured puritan, of Swift with his despairing cry: "Celia, Celia, Celia shits." If he had ever been confronted by the proposition, I think Russell would have been abashed to explain how a practicing gynecologist could ever remain in love. This is a problem that afflicts surely only a fraction of the population, although transient symptoms of it disturb the sort of genteel lady, surprisingly common in America, who never retires to the bathroom without turning on the water tap.

Russell himself has charted in exhausting detail the peaks and pits of his love affairs, and the smooth and rocky paths in between. And at least two wives and several other ladies have been only too eager to offer their own voluminous testimony in support, and often in defiance, of his affidavits. It is a fate that the most honest man should not wish on himself, and the history of it has no decent place in a memoir of this sort. But after a fifty-eight-year war with the demon of sex, he managed a touching truce. At the end of 1952, when he was eighty, he married Edith Finch, yet another Bryn Mawr graduate. He wrote a poem to her which graces, in a photostatic copy of his aged scrawl, the title page of the first volume of his autobiography. It would be charitable to call it banal, and a half-literate person coming on it without a signature might shrewdly attribute it to Robert W. Service or Ella Wheeler Wilcox:

> Through the long years
> I sought peace.
> I found ecstasy, I found anguish,
> I found madness,
> I found loneliness.
> I found the solitary pain
> That gnaws the heart,
> But peace I did not find.
> Now, old and near my end,
> I have known you,
> And, knowing you,
> I have found both ecstasy and peace.
> I know rest.
> After so many lonely years,
> I know what life and love may be.
> Now, if I sleep,
> I shall sleep fulfilled.

The evidence of both parties, and of all the friends and onlookers who saw them together, testifies that it was far and away the happiest of his marriages. But he had not resolved his old tussle with "Marriage and Morals." It seems more probable that, like legions of ordinary people, he had discovered that in old age a serene companionship with the other sex becomes for the first time possible. Once passion is spent, morality comes a little easier.

In the end, what we are left with is a towering malcontent, the last of the Whigs, whose aristocratic heritage and contradictions of personality will not easily accommodate the usual labels of Rightist, Leftist, Socialist, Liberal. With his liberal belief in rational reform, his Socialist belief in radical change, his conservative scorn for violence and disorder, his love of "leisured culture," his discomfort in the presence of working people (which today would be taken to contradict his approval of equality of opportunity), he is by now impossible to pin down as either a political or social type. And apart from accepting the title of Socialist (usually at odds with any Socialist government in being), he would not have wished to be pinned down. His considerable vanity, for one thing, resisted it. But what made him wary of swallowing whole any prescribed political program was his fierce independence of thought and his unsleeping passion—the claim of no party and no class—for the liberty of the subject, however high or low. He has been the great libertarian of our age, and it is an age in which, in the Western world, there is an almost routine confusion between liberty and equality.

Sometime, somewhere, Russell sweated to believe, the rational man would make a decent world of his instincts. This is, of course, not a new conviction. It is held, as a dizzy hope, by all evangelists. But whereas the autobiographies of John the Baptist or Billy Graham might be very dull indeed, Russell gave the struggle to make it come true the dimensions of a Greek tragedy. For he was at once a first-class intellect, a man of unyielding, if cantankerous, honesty, and the possessor of one of the master styles of the English language. It is the last of these gifts that may ensure the bystander, even decades from now, an unflagging fascination with his life. For his style gives charm to many a frailty, makes the world over every day in the light of his intelligence and irony, converts political crusades into cantos from Milton and exchanges of learned correspondence and lovers' flutings into episodes as enchanting as sonatas.

The great, and maddening, thing about him is that he would not give in—to prudence or a party line or cynicism, or, I'm afraid, to simple horse sense. He would go to prison for a principle in his forties; weather public scorn in his eighties for urging the banning of the bomb or proclaiming Kennedy and Khrushchev as villains; and in his ninety-eighth year—two days before he died—feel duty bound to protest against Israeli air raids on Egypt, knowing full well he would thereby alienate yet another band of recent admirers: "The aggression committed by Israel must be condemned, not only because no State has the right to annex foreign territory, but because every expansion is also an experiment to discover how much more aggression the world will tolerate. . . . We are frequently told that we must sympathize with Israel because of the suffering of the Jews in Europe at the hands of the Nazis. I see in this suggestion no reason to perpetuate any suffering. What Israel is doing today cannot be condoned, and to invoke the horrors of the past to justify those of the present is gross hypocrisy." It was the last thing he wrote or dictated.

He raged against the dying of the light of reason in human affairs but more against the greed, cowardice, hatreds, and injustices of his fellowmen, of whom, from time to time, he greatly feared he might be one.

VI

HUMPHREY BOGART
Epitaph for a Tough Guy

IN THE FALL OF 1952, we were coming to the end of the Eisenhower-Stevenson presidential campaign, and I joined the Stevenson train for its last lap through New England.

There comes a time in every campaign when the roving reporter, almost as much as the candidates, screams for surcease. He loses all sense of time, place, a daily pattern of life, or a routine of civility with his fellowmen. There had always been the clanking monotony of the campaign train, swaying through plains and mountains and deserts while hunched-over foursomes clutching poker hands peer between the slats of the club car and say, "Is this still Texas?" But in the 1950s there had been added the peculiar nightmare of the campaign *plane*, which robs the candidate of all excuses that he cannot get to Oklahoma City, say, for an early breakfast rally after a night speech in Miami. Even more than the train, the campaign plane obliterates any continental sense of the country whose variety you are supposed to be remarking and reporting on. The engines throb and writhe and fall. There is no light but darkness visible up front as two yellow blobs fall on the notebooks of the only two reporters who are awake and sentient. All the others are sprawled like drunken cattle rustlers in a B film. Whistles blow through yellow teeth; gargles trip over a uvula; baritone groans come lurching up from an esophagus. It would be a disgusting scene if it were not for its overwhelming pathos. Here are the Rover Boys, the unfooled agency men, and the crew of enforced buddies who have been assigned since the nomination to this candidate and no other. They have counted noses in Chicago, pondered the Polish vote in Pittsburgh, the old folks' vote in Florida; they have alerted their readers to watch for the swamping of the liberal vote in Northern California by the conservative vote of Los Angeles and San Diego counties. They have weighed trends everywhere. But the anxieties that nag them are the unreturned raincoat borrowed in Oregon, the plastic food at every rally, the shirt they've worn for four days, and the fact that the train or plane begins to smell of rotten apples. Most of all, they have come to look with glazed eyes on the candidates as the club bores. A presidential candidate may start out bristling with energy and exhaling idealism. But after the first forty stops he has to strain for sincerity and to pump up the indignation. Of all the politicians I have followed on the stump, only Lloyd George and Roosevelt could make speeches in the last weeks sound like rhetoric newly felt and believed in. (This does not mean they were finer men. They had more consummate techniques and could maintain outrageous promises without the flicker of an eyelid.) Even a campaign that begins as a crusade ends as a vaudeville act. The same rousing perorations in the same words, the identical jokes are trotted out five times a day till the reporters are blearyeyed with cynicism.

WE WERE WELL INTO THIS STAGE by the time Stevenson had made his big speech in Boston and taken the train south to wind up the campaign at a night rally in Harlem. Very early on the first morning when a white fog was barely moving from the valleys, and wisps of smoke were rising from little piles of burning leaves, we came to a halt at some village in Rhode Island. No more than a score of the locals shuffled up to the rear of the train. A few boys were larking around on a hillside. An urchin was settled like a frog on a telegraph pole. The local county chairman, or whoever, came out on the observation platform and bellowed into a microphone about the pride and pleasure of Rhode Islanders in welcoming "the next President of the United States." After a speech leaden with clichés, he was very proud indeed to introduce two fine Americans who had come along to proclaim their faith in Adlai Stevenson. He announced them, and they weren't there. Minions ducked into the train, the chairman gave reassuring nods ("They're here all right"), and a few hearty claps from inside brought them on. They were Humphrey Bogart and his wife, Lauren Bacall. A small cheer went up from the villagers, and the boys on the hill hoisted invisible tommy guns and chattered "rat-a-tat-tat!"

Bacall flashed her engaging grin and waved, while Bogart had to be pushed into view. With his coffee-colored complexion and bloodshot eyes, he looked, as always, like the old crony roused from a heavy night, though in truth he had behaved impeccably, slept well, and kept to himself in his compartment. He gave a

couple of nervous nods, waved once at the gang on the
hill, and backed off to make way for the Governor.
Stevenson, a little puffy himself, allowed it was kind of
"you-all" to come out so early to greet a Democrat
(they had probably done two hours of farm chores by
that time) and went into what we called the "falling
leaves" speech. It was Republican country and he knew
it, but "let me say to the good Republicans of New
England, there is always a light in the Democratic
window and a warm welcome awaiting you in the
Democratic Party....And now I notice, in this
beautiful fall, that Republican votes are falling like the
autumn leaves."

I was standing on the track and caught Bogart's eye.
The faintest shrug of the eyebrows and a lick of the
upper lip seemed to say, "What d'you expect the poor
bastard to say at seven in the morning?" This was my
first contact, if that's what it could be called, with
Bogart. Stevenson spread-eagled his arms and gave his
golliwog grin, and we all bundled back aboard the train
and were off.

I was pretty sure the Bogarts were not dedicated
readers of the (then) *Manchester Guardian* and had
never heard of me. But Bacall stopped me, as I was
going by their compartment, and wondered if I wasn't
the guy who was going to emcee the first weekly ninety-
minute television show, which indeed I was. They
invited me to drop in later for a drink. I was very
flattered. As a film critic long ago, I had been vaguely
aware of Bogart in his earliest appearances as an
uncomfortable leading man in such forgettable items
as *A Devil with Women* and *Love Affair*, but I had
followed him with relish, as something quite new, after
The Petrified Forest and into his glory days in
Casablanca, To Have and Have Not, The Big Sleep,
and *Key Largo*. In the last three, he had had as his

leading lady the girl with the honey-colored eyes and the baby-leopard slouch who was now his wife. So that to the curious animal magnetism of Bogart, as of an attractive armadillo, was now added the pleasure of beauty mating the beast.

The first impression was that of a subdued and friendly tough in his wrong element, like *The Streets of San Francisco*'s Lieutenant Stone being asked to take a seat in the Morgan Library. It is a superficial impression, no doubt, but one that showed how hard it was to see Bogart, the man, through the glittering shell of his film character. Perhaps he was a little nervous about having yielded to his wife's insistence that they get out on the road and flaunt their allegiance to Stevenson. The Communist hunt was then in full cry. And five years before, when the McCarthy era was incubating in the congressional hearings on Communist subversion in the film industry, Bogart had flown to Washington to defend the right of ten "unfriendly" Hollywood witnesses to think and say "anything they damn please." (He was aghast to discover that several of them were down-the-line Communists coolly exploiting the protection of the First and Fifth Amendments to the Constitution. He had thought they were just freewheeling anarchists, like himself.) Now, in 1952, Richard Nixon, Eisenhower's running mate, was making very little distinction between liberal Democrats—from Secretary of State Acheson on down—and actual traitors. Most studio heads, however much they might deplore this scurrility in private, were publicly inclined to share the suspicions of their fellow Californian Nixon, and when it was murmured around the lots that an open embrace of Stevenson might possibly weaken the bonds of a film contract, there was a glad rush of stars all too eager to be seen liking Ike. Bogart and his wife packed their bags and went off with Stevenson.

I would learn later that Bogart's correctness and modesty aboard the train—appearing when he was told to, bowing briefly, and seeing that the limelight never veered from the candidate—had nothing whatever to do with fear or timidity. He was simply doing his bit in a strange milieu and minding his manners.

As the train ran through southern Massachusetts, I had wind of a story that promised a climax to the campaign as hair-raising as the disclosure, in 1884, that Grover Cleveland, the Democratic candidate, had an illegitimate son. It seemed that the Democratic National Committee had somehow secured a copy of a letter from General Marshall to Eisenhower, when he was supreme commander of NATO, more or less commanding him to stay with his command, and his wife, and forget a young Englishwoman, who had been his wartime chauffeuse and, apparently, his mistress. While we were aboard the Stevenson train, Senator Joseph McCarthy was to make a speech in Chicago of a virulence verging on libel. The Democrats had got an advance copy of the speech and secretly warned the Republican high command that if it were delivered in that form, they would publicize the Marshall letter.* When I told this story to the Bogarts, his eyes boggled in disbelief. I boggled back, for I guessed that to a character so marinated in corruption, adultery would be the most trivial sin in the decalogue. But Bogart was genuinely shocked.

That moment of shock on the train was the first hint I had that what we were dealing with here were two characters, one fictional, the other private, almost as sharply defined as Chaplin, the man, and Charlie, the

---

* McCarthy's actual speech was toned down almost to the point of refinement.

tramp. There was the movie Bogart, a character at once
repellent and fascinating; and the complex private
man. I imagine I would have given no more thought to
the puzzle had the Bogarts not asked me soon
afterward to visit them in Hollywood and made clear,
in the unspoken way of people warming to strangers,
that we were to be friends from then on. From the
afternoon of that first drink till the day of his death, I
found him an original quite unlike any other human
being I have known. And what remained engrossing
about him was the duality of his character. Duality is
perhaps a misleading word. It implies a split, or
running conflict, between the movie character (the
tough) and the private character. Whereas it is more
likely that the movie character—and the reflection of it
in Bogart's more raucous public behavior—sprang
from a rebellion against the gentility of his parents and
the life they had expected him to lead. For the first
surprise to the film fan looking into his origins is the
extreme contrast with what you had been led to expect. In a guessing game with people otherwise
knowledgeable about the theater and the movies, I
have often heard it suggested that Humphrey Bogart
was probably a studio invention to obliterate some
unpronounceable Polish or Russian name. But the
reality is that he was christened Humphrey DeForest
Bogart, that his mother was a fashionable portrait
painter of socialite children, and that his father, a
successful physician with the even more formidable
Waspish name of Dr. Belmont DeForest Bogart, had
an income from a family inheritance, a country house
in the Finger Lakes, and a brownstone house on upper
Riverside Drive, a New York address which—when
Park Avenue had railroad tracks running up the
middle of it—was the very seal of upper-middle-class
respectability.

213

The young Bogart went for eight years to an Episcopal school with rituals leaning heavily toward Rome and a code of discipline leaning heavily toward Sparta. He then was sent to Andover, where the omens of his coming lapse from gentility were abundant. He kept mostly to himself; he was an obstinate nonstudent; he failed in everything and after a year was thrown out for "irreverence" and "uncontrollable high spirits." At this point, his father must have abandoned his wistful hope that the boy would go on to Yale. Instead, he enlisted in the Navy and was ready for ship duty two weeks after the First World War was over. After that, he was intended—but not by himself—for a business career and eventually drifted, through some actor neighbors, into the theater, where he started as a company manager, and in the usual way got to speak oneliners. That he would ever earn a living from acting is something that the critics, and I should guess most of his friends, would have betted heavily against. His appearances went usually unnoticed in a series of footling country-house comedies which kept up the presense that the First World War had merely grazed the Edwardian era. When he had the misfortune to be mentioned, it was for "trenchant bad acting" or for a performance that Alexander Woollcott wrote "could be mercifully described as inadequate." Only the most addicted playgoers could have learned to recognize the dark-haired juvenile who loped through French windows wearing tails or a dinner jacket and seemed to be cast for life as a Riviera fixture. Once, it is said, he appeared in an ascot and a blue blazer and tossed off the invitation that was to become immortal: "Tennis, anyone?" Probably he did not coin the phrase, but he glorified the type that used it, if lithe young men with brown eyes and no discoverable talent can ever be said to go to glory, onstage or off.

And yet ten or more years later he gave currency to

another phrase with which the small fry of the English-speaking world brought the neighborhood sneak to heel: "Drop the gun, Looey!" Could both these characters be Bogart, the cryptic Hemingway tough, the huddled man in the trench coat who singed the bad and the beautiful with the smoke he exhaled from his nostrils? Could any actor, no matter how lucky in his parts, how wide the gamut of his ambition, swing so successfully between the poles of make-believe represented by "Tennis, anyone?" and "Drop the gun, Looey!"? He could and did. It is time to try to explain the inexplicable.

It had to do, I think, with the lucky (for him) coincidence of the coming of the sound film and the collapse of a social structure whose romantic leads Bogart had so inadequately impersonated.

From the very creation of the movies, the directors exploited motion, the novelty that fetched the rubes, in train wrecks, Indian attacks, and the ultimate commotion of the chase. But whenever human emotions were involved, they acted on the error that they were photographing a stage play. "Acting," everybody knew, entailed the broad gesture, the lilting or trenchant cadence, the cameo stance, the human form seen as a cardboard cutout of certain elemental emotions—greed, shame, pride, penitence, humility, ardor—all filmed at the proper remove of the proscenium arch and composed within its frame. The invention of the medium shot and the close-up, far from challenging the actors to quiet down, made them all the more eager to demonstrate their ability to mime in silence the agonies and ecstasies of their trade. So the early producers, without a second thought, hired stage actors, and the biggest salaries went to the biggest stage names. By getting Sarah Bernhardt they thought they were getting the supreme feast of acting. But any year after the invention of sound, film audiences could see her only as a figure of fun, a dumb creature jerking her sawdust heart around in a puppet world.

The sound film, after succumbing for a couple of years or so to the old prejudice about what constituted acting, took the audience out of the theater and into a living room, in which the actors were more like us and moved at the distance of ordinary conversation. The point came up once when we took the Bogarts to a Broadway play, a modern adaptation of a Greek legend, in which the leading player was an English actor with distinguished stage credentials. Bogart was unimpressed by him mainly, I now think, because we were seated on the second row and could see not only the kohl-rimmed eyes, the suspended gestures, and an occasional spume of spittle, but also a sprinkle of little rhinestone stars sewn onto the actor's jockstrap, a detail that immoderately amused Bogart and brought withering frowns and shushes from his wife, who threatened after the first act to separate us, as you do with twins larking in church. Bogart, explaining his coolness toward the English star, recalled how, when sound came in, there was a panic search for "actors who could speak." To the producers, who were then either former stage impresarios or immigrants who had had their own troubles with the language, people who could speak meant Englishmen.

If this tradition had kept up, and the sound film gone undiscovered for another decade or so, I doubt that Bogart would ever have been heard of. For he was clearly uncomfortable "projecting" as a stage actor. He seemed to possess no vanity; he had a shrinking dislike of ostentation and a total absence of that narcissism that above anything else drives people into acting. It may well be why his first stay in Hollywood doomed him to small, asinine parts in trivial films and forced him to head back to New York and abandon a scene he was never going to make. But by now acting, for better or worse, was his only trade. It was the trough of the Depression, Dr. Bogart's fortunes had been badly hit, and Bogart was on Broadway again in two or three failing plays, in which, however, since the hair was thinner and the lisp thicker, he began to be cast—and recognized—as Broadway's automatic cad, wastrel, ne'er-do-well. He was just as old as the century, and by the mid-thirties he was getting to be a little too scarred for a juvenile. He was ready to fade into the kind of feature player who, because he has worked at his job to acquire a dependable technique, will never be out of a job but will never star in anything.

At this point, in 1934, he went at one bound into the crude prototype of the character for which he would become renowned. Robert Sherwood had written *The Petrified Forest*, a melodrama heavy-laden with moralizing, but with one character in it, a sad, forthright, listless killer, whose reality cut like a knife through the butter of the surrounding philosophy. Against the advice of his friends, who remembered Bogart from his tennis racketeering, Sherwood picked the aging juvenile with the scar, the odd lisp, and the look of implied derision. Bogart was an immediate success and was soon whipped out to Hollywood for the movie version. And that lead to *Dead End* and the glory road of the gangster hero, or—as we should now say—antihero. Bogart put it all down to luck, which is a change from the actor's steady refusal to admit that the stars in their courses are nearly always set by the casting director. Spencer Tracy was dully cast as a bum, a doughboy, even a lover until somebody guessed that an affectionate Portuguese fisherman was closer to the raw material. Merle Oberon's battle with the adjective "sloe-eyed" was a stalemate until she was, surprisingly, glamorized into naturalness. A new view of an old face was all it took to change Wallace Beery from a slant-eyed villain into a lovable cuss, to turn Myrna Loy from an "inscrutable," as the word is understood in Oriental melodramas, into a chin-up wife for William Powell, himself transformed by the same insight from a gunman into a teasing combination of smooth operator and faithful spouse.

I have called the killer in *The Petrified Forest* a "crude" prototype of the essential Bogart soon to be distilled, because Sherwood was a stagy writer. (Graham Greene, reviewing the movie in England, chided Sherwood for his inability, in Henry James's prescriptive phrase, to "dramatize, dramatize," for his fatal inclination to see a play as "ideas being expressed, 'significant,' cosmic ideas" so that "everyone works hard to try to give the illusion that the Whole of Life is symbolized in the Arizona filling station. But life itself, which crept in during the opening scene, embarrassed perhaps at hearing itself so explicitly discussed, crept out again, leaving us only with the symbols, the pasteboard desert, the stunted cardboard studio trees.") Much of this wooden self-consciousness was built into the movie script—it is an appalling film to see today—and if Bogart had not had subtleties inside him itching to get out, he might have rocketed and faded, as a one-shot star. He was now cast as a box-office bad man, but within two or three years, by the time of *Black Legion* and *Kid Galahad*, Otis Ferguson—the most gifted film critic of my time—wrote that "you had the feeling that he was writing his own parts." This is as handsome a compliment as you can pay to a movie actor, for it signifies that he is at one with the medium in a way that few distinguished stage actors ever manage to be: he had blossomed into something that, in the early thirties, was quite new in the world of make-believe—the actor who didn't seem to act but *behaved*.

This professional maturity, his being suddenly and permanently at home with the trade in which he had for so long stumbled, coincided with the end of the postwar era (what Westbrook Pegler called the Era of Wonderful Nonsense) and the beginning of the prewar era of anxiety, one of those ideological wrenches which, in destroying a social structure, suddenly date more symbols of it than philandering socialites, "stout fellas," and courtesans, not least the prevailing fashion in romantic actors. It is fair to guess that far back in the Coward-Lonsdale era, Bogart was always his own man. He no doubt stood in the wings in his blue blazer chuckling over the inanities onstage, and he would have been the first man to question that youth ever deposited its bloom on him. But for a long time, it obscured, in a sleek complexion, bold eyes, and a lid of black hair, his essential and very individual character and its marvelous adaptability to one of the more glamorous neuroses of the incoming day and age: that of the hard-bitten "private eye," the neutral skeptic in a world exploding with crusades and the treachery they invite. He probably had no notion, in his endless strolls across the stage drawing rooms of the twenties, that he was being saved and soured by Time to become the romantic democratic answer to Hitler's new order. Such calculations belong to social historians, not to their subject. Not, certainly, to an actor who had always pretended to no sort of evangelism, who had horsed around town and had his troubles with the bartender's tab, and who had always been grateful to take any part for which his dark and glossy appearance qualified him. He made a boast of his willingness to nestle in the camouflage of any fictional type that came his way, provided the manager paid him and left him to himself.

He was never earnest about the choice of parts "worthy" of him, as most newly discovered stars tend to be. I doubt he would ever have joined group theaters or studios dedicated to the purifying or solemnizing of the mummer's art. He was temperamentally disinclined to identify the actor with a priest or a social reformer, at a time when Hollywood and New York were hoarse with actors asserting the need to synchronize an acting method with "a social conscience." Bogart spoke his mind very freely on this, as on most other subjects, and he was consequently not idolized by aesthetes or by the New Deal young as a serious actor. At least, not in his own country. Which, long before the Bogart cult, produced a comic irony. It is a hazard peculiar to cultists in the arts—that is to say, to avowed members of the intelligentsia—that unless they keep their transatlantic signals open and alert, they will tend to canonize foreign talents that are rejected on the home ground as commercial hacks. There was a delightful period in the late thirties and early forties when American intellectuals yearned for a native naturalistic actor as mighty as Jean Gabin. Their counterparts in Paris were meanwhile lamenting the early demise of Gabin as a "serious" talent and panting over Bogart for what the critic of *Le Monde* called his "vitalisme, tendre et profond."

I once mentioned this awesome Gallic reputation to Bogart, and he was greatly amused by it. Although he privately described himself as "Democrat in politics, Episcopalian by upbringing, dissenter by disposition," he looked on acting as a trade like any other, though one calling for some craft and considerable discipline. He was always touchy about his pride not in his artistry but in his competence, and competence was something

220

he greatly admired in any field, from writing to seamanship, drinking to statesmanship. He measured all his fellow workers by the test of professionalism, and a professional was a man who can do his best work when he doesn't feel like it. Being also a clear-minded man of deep and quite stubborn convictions, he was something of a freak in the Hollywood factory in knowing where his craft ended and where his private life of politics should take over without let or hindrance. His admiration of Roosevelt, his steady contempt for Senator Joseph McCarthy, his mulish determination to stay in a restaurant till dawn if a drinking fit was on him had no more to do with his acceptance or rejection of a part than a trucking company's contract with a newspaper publisher depends on the political strips of the editorials.

In a fuzzier man, or a more cunning one, this separation of the citizen and the craftsman could have been a very handy sort of cowardice. Bogart was quite clear about the point where his conscience could not bow to his fame. He once sailed into the Newport, California, harbor and took his skipper along with him to the yacht club bar. An official beckoned him aside and intimated that a respectable yacht club was no place to bring his "paid hands." Bogart called for his bar check and on the back of it wrote out his resignation. The effect was hardly instantaneous on the board, which, for all I know, may never have changed a rule since the time of Canute. But it changed this one a month or two later by a majority vote.

The yacht club official was probably suffering from a delusion that most film fans would find hard to shake—namely, the assumption that the private Bogart was the same amiable, conscienceless tough as his movie self. On a nighttime stroll up Fifth Avenue, he was once complaining to me that he could not walk the streets of New York without having truck drivers and assorted brats spring their forefingers and give him the "ah-ah-ah-rat-a-tat-tat" tommy-gun treatment. Within minutes, a wholesome young cop testing store locks at two in the morning moved up from behind. "Everything all right, Mr. Bogart?" he said. Everything was fine, and Bogart sighed after his retreating bulk: "It does no good. I haven't played a gangster or a dick in nine years."

But this was his most famous self. The two-faced cynic who robbed the banker and the grafter with equal grace, who was sometimes a heel and sometimes a big-city stand-in for the United States cavalry, but who was always the derisive foe of the law in its official, pompous forms. The enjoyment of this character from Glasgow to Singapore was assured by the supporting artistic fact that here was a universal type of our rebellious age but one that never appeared in life quite so perfect, never quite so detached in its malice, so inured to corruption, so self-assured in its social stance before the pretentious, the diffident, and the evil. It would be tempting—and the French have undoubtedly been tempted—to write of the Bogart character as the archetype of the Outsider, but he packed the more explosive social threat of the Insider gone sour, all the more convincing because the disillusion grew from his own background and the unknown cause of his protest against it.

Because Bogart was seen by more millions than had ever read Dickens or Poe or John Gay, it is tempting to say that he is a romantic hero inconceivable in any time but ours. But the previous paragraph, with few changes, would do as a description of Robin Hood and more accurately of Macheath in *The Beggar's Opera*, which is indeed a terrifying celebration of the way the criminal hero is partner with the government itself in

the exploitation of the law: an allegory of Watergate.
Nearly thirty years ago, Jacob Bronowski wrote a play
and a preface (*The Face of Violence*) which traces "the
love of violence [as] the ancient and symbolic gesture
of man against the constraints of society" and shows
that what is permanently fascinating about detective
thrillers is not, as academics like to declare, their
intellectual puzzles but the crime itself, which we all
secretly itch to perform.

But for our purpose we can say that the Bogart film
character was the most developed popular expression
of the tough guy who was equally fascinating whether
the plot said he was the hero or the villain. This is a
bold advance on the Victorian convention of the
detective as a mind superior to that of the regular
officer of the law and therefore the better able to
uphold it. I would say that Bogart was simply the most
vivid impersonation of the character invented by
Dashiell Hammett and Raymond Chandler, and that
his immense popularity through the late 1930s and on
into the forties, and his emergence among the young in
the fifties and sixties as a cult hero, were due in the
main to the rise of Hitler.

The success of violence, in our politics and our
cities, has forced historians to trace the crackup in
bourgeois society to a time well before the world
Depression that exacerbated it. In fact, to the
Edwardians. A distinguished diplomatic historian has
said that the merit of the popular British television
series *Upstairs, Downstairs* was to confirm a wealth of
late-nineteenth-century and early-twentieth-century
documents in showing that it was Upstairs, not
Downstairs, that cracked. And if this is so, it is no
accident that Bogart can now be seen as a direct
descendant of Sherlock Holmes as are most fictional
private detectives invented since Conan Doyle, in a

moment of unconscious social perception, cast the original mold. Sherlock Holmes could not exist if his creator and his audience did not share the solid Dickensian premise that "the law is an ass." He was born fully grown as a metropolitan eccentric ("the detective," wrote Bronowski, "does not visit the suburbs, only the copper pounds his beat there, and every midnight reader knows that the copper is ridiculous"). He is the antithesis of the respectable families that gobbled him up: a depressed, eccentric bachelor of vast, odd knowledge, whose intelligence is poised over the plot like a dagger which, in the moment of resolution, plunges to the heart of it. This is the elementary recipe for all the moderns, from Peter Wimsey—the interesting variation of a manic rather than a depressed bachelor—through Perry Mason to Philip Marlowe. Where Holmes knew the soil classification of the Home Counties, Bogart—sharing an unfriendly drink with Sidney Greenstreet—sees a ship slink by on the horizon and calls off the full-load displacement, overall length, gun caliber, and muzzle velocity. Holmes possessed an uncanny sense of the whereabouts of distressed gentlewomen and had memorized the Paddington train timetable against the day of their rescue. Bogart knows all about hotels from Yokohama to New York: the tactical geography of suites, connecting doors, and fire escapes, how to confuse the room clerk and evade the house dick, determine the clientele by a glance around the lobby, know who is up to no good and where she is likely to be.

The field maneuvers may be different from those in Holmes's day, and the villain is a little more socially mobile, but since then we have not changed the three essential ingredients of the private eye. He must be a bachelor, with the bachelor's harum-scarum availability at all hours (William Powell's marriage to Myrna "Nora" Loy, a wistful concession to the family trade, fooled nobody). He must have an inconspicuous fund of curious knowledge, which in the end is always crucially relevant. He must despise, pity at least, the official guardians of the law.

Of course, the twentieth century has grafted some interesting personality changes on the original. Holmes was an eccentric in the Victorian sense, a man with queer hobbies—cocaine was lamentable but pardonably bohemian—whose social code was essentially that of the ruling classes. He was, in a way, the avenging squire of the underworld ready to administer a horsewhipping to the outcasts who were never privileged by birth to receive it from their fathers, Bogart is a displaced person whose present respectability is uncertain, a classless but well-contained vagabond who is not going to be questioned about where he came from or where he is going. ("I came to Casablanca for the waters." "Mr. Rick, zere are no waters in Casablanca." "I was misinformed.")

As a Victorian bachelor-hero, Holmes must be presumed to be asexual. Bogart too is a lone wolf but with a new and equal stress on the noun. His general view of women implies that he was brought up, sexually speaking, no earlier than the twenties. Hence, his is unshockable and offhand, and, one gathers, a very devil with the women who is saved from absurdity by never having time to prove it. ("Sorry, angel, I have a pressing date with a fat man.") Unlike Holmes, he cannot claim even the castle of a carefully cluttered set of rooms. He is always on the move, and his only domestic base is a fairly seedy hotel bedroom with an unmade bed (this is called audience identification, and to tell the truth is the sort of independent base of operations most college boys and many rueful husbands would like to have). Yet somehow, somewhere, in his baffling past he learned the habits of the *haut monde*. And his audience is quietly flattered by the revelation that a sudden call to dine at the Ritz will find him shaved and natty and handling the right knives with easy boredom.

It is a gorgeous fantasy, fulfilling more desires in the audience than a Freudian could shake a totem at, and it was given an entertaining dry run in the appearances of Warren William as Perry Mason. But it was always thought of as B-film material until Bogart turned it into box office, a change that can be simply attributed to what Peter Ustinov has called his "enormous presence," the simple, inexplicable characteristic of natural stars: you cannot take your eyes off them. (No one in the history of the movies had made smoking a cigarette a more deadly and fascinating thing to watch—and deadly, alas, in the end to him.) Why we couldn't take our eyes off Bogart had much to do, as I have suggested, with the coincidence of the fictional character with what was repressed or socially impermissible in his own. But, as an historical break, his great popularity blossomed after his graduation from gangster parts just when parliamentary Europe was caving in to gangsters on a grand scale. And with *Casablanca*, the legend flowered. Nathaniel Benchley had pointed out the god-sent luck of its timing. It had been made after Pearl Harbor but before American forces had played any independent part in the war. Then, "on November 8, 1942, Allied forces landed on the coast of French North Africa, specifically at Oran, Algiers, and Casablanca. It was as though Warner Brothers had planned the invasion; eighteen days later, on Thanksgiving Day, *Casablanca* opened in New York. As though that weren't enough, its general release came on January 23, 1943, in the middle of the conference between Roosevelt and Churchill at Casablanca. Because of wartime security the conference couldn't be publicized at the time, but its subsequent news stories did nothing whatsoever to harm the picture."

There was nothing now to offend the most respectable suburban patriot in a hero who used the gangster's means to achieve our ends. And this character was suddenly very precious in the age of violence, for it satisfied a quiet, desperate need of the engulfed ordinary citizen. When Hitler was acting out scripts more brutal and obscene than anything dreamed of by Chicago's North Side or Warner Brothers, Bogart was the only possible antagonist likely to outwit him and survive. What was needed was no knight of the boudoir, no Ronald Colman or Leslie Howard (whose movie careers compensatingly slumped) but a conniver as subtle as Goebbels. Bogart was the very tough gent required, a murderously bland neutral who we knew, if the Germans didn't, would in the end be on our side.

More than any other character he was to play, this one fitted Bogart's own like a glove. His subsequent portrayals of straightforward heroes, or even of straightforward psychopaths (*The Caine Mutiny, In a Lonely Place*), show the strain of deliberate "acting" and can be mercifully overlooked. It was in the character of Rick, the nightclub owner in *Casablanca*, that the audience saw once for all Bogart behaving as a decent approximation to the melancholy man whose wryness was the mask of an incorruptibility he mocked. And it brings us back to Humphrey Bogart, the son of Dr. Bogart, who was thrown out of school, did a stint in the Navy, fumbled around the theater, and eventually became the big Hollywood star.

It was inevitable that the press should create its own

saleable brand of the Bogart "personality." He did
drink a good deal and get into occasional restaurant
fights. He tolerated, even fattened, the newspaper
myth of a locker-room tough guy. When his marriage
to a redoubtable blonde, Mayo Methot, was failing,
the press spread the word that he was living out his
screen character in a running series of marital brawls.
"Battling Bogart," the columnists called him. "Battling
Bogart!" groaned Clifton Webb, one of his oldest
friends. "Why, any woman could walk all over him.
The man's a softie and—I might add—a very gallant
one."

In most of us, the contradictions of character settle
down among friends into a general atmosphere of
tolerance and shared fun, with the lamentations over
our irritant traits mentioned in private when the party's
over. In Bogart, the contradictions were evidently so
gross that people who loathed him could never credit
how anyone could love him. And vice versa. Some
people saw nothing but a moody drunk, a barfly given
to random practical jokes and spasms of sadism, a
cynic with more than a touch of paranoia leading to
tasteless verbal assaults on anyone who conveyed a
hint of pomp or authority or the lacier attributes of
homosexuality. Others, who knew him well, found him
gentle, gallant, modest, full of an indulgent or rueful
humor, courteous with strangers, quietly and acutely
sensitive to the plight of guests who were shy or being
left out.

Quite apart from noticing his behavior on the
Stevenson train, I was prejudiced in his favor by one or
two young actors who had been hustled out to
Hollywood on the strength of a Broadway success.
They had gone to Bogart, as to their resident consul
general, to learn how to domesticate themselves in the
Hollywood jungle. He gave them two excellent bits of

advice (which they did not act upon): "Take the big part, but hold off the big house and Cadillac, or you'll be in hock to the studio for the rest of your life"; and "The only point in making money is so you can tell some big producer to go screw himself." If these fledgling stars checked these maxims with old inhabitants, they were usually told that Bogart was an incurable scoffer, a bred-in-the-bone iconoclast.

His iconoclasm was, I believe, the rather gaudy mask of a conservatism that embarrassed him. Any rebel, said Bernard Shaw, has an obligation to replace the conventions he destroys with better ones. It doesn't take a hellion more than a few years to discover that this is not going to happen. A mark of many successful revolutionaries is their distaste for construction projects once the smoke has cleared. Lesser rebels—as we have seen in the settling wake of the storms of the late 1960s—tend to fall back with sheepish respect on the code of their elders and mentors, the first code they learned before they learned to ridicule it. We have all seen a parody of this mechanism in the moralizing of aging rakes, whose later puritanism takes on the bigotry of conversion. I don't think Bogart had the temperament of a rake, but he had some nagging compulsion to put up a show of masculinity. He was the last man you'd expect, from his outward manner, to have the pedestrian old-school virtues: loyalty to friends, respect for the old, a distaste for conspicuous wealth, for gossip, for boasting—to name no others. Yet he had them, knew them to be old-fashioned, and kept up his prestige among the young Turks by cockily asserting their opposite. Hollywood's "progress" over twenty years, he once remarked, could be measured by the fact that "I came out here with one suit and everybody thought I was a bum; when Brando came out with one sweat shirt, the town drooled over him."

229

He was very vocal about the pretentiousness of the new school of realistic actors who must "feel" a character before they start to play it. "Acting," Bogart insisted, "is a job like any other. It takes practice to be good at it. After that, you learn your lines, concentrate on nothing else, get dressed and go home." However, I think his real complaint about the "method" actors was they they wore blue jeans and windbreakers.

I'm afraid he would take it with a snort if he could hear me saying it, though it is nothing but the truth, that he had the impulses of a gentleman but was born late enough to squirm over the vocabulary that normally expresses them. I can hardly hear him saying that marriage is a firm contract and that fidelity is no more than a married man's duty. But there seems no doubt that he acted on the principle. When, in his last year, he had been confined to his house for many months, people used to urge his wife, Lauren Bacall, to get out in the evenings once he was tucked away. He urged her himself, in an offhand way. But he was secretly proud that she didn't. And, just before he died, not so secret about it. A friend remarked, not really knowing what answer to expect, that Betty had been out only half a dozen evenings in ten months. He said, almost casually, "She's my wife and my nurse. So she stays home. Maybe that's the way you tell the ladies from the broads in this town."

One is always reading, in obituaries, of some bold good man who could not abide cant and fearlessly denounced it. Bogart never bothered to denounce it since, no matter how meek its disguise, it was as plainly offensive to him as a bad smell. And his hypersensitiveness to the faintest aura of pomp made him an impossible man to make up to, to cozen or impress. Many first acquaintances were dropped at once when, out of shyness probably, they tried to adopt some of the Bogart bluster in the hope of showing right away that they were his sort. One of his own sort was enough for him. He took to many unlikely types and immediately tended to admire people who, however quaint, were nobody but themselves. He did not require a woman to appear knowing, an Englishman to rough up his accent, or anyone to buddy up to him by telling a so-called dirty story. This last gesture was a fatal mistake: Bogart detested dirty stories and shut up like a clam. You could say also that he was socially difficult in that he was impatient of compliments and perfunctory praise. He had the deadly insight that one meets with in some drunks (and that one hopes not to meet with in most schizophrenics) who are beginning to get troublesome and whom you hope to appease with cordial approaches. Such psychics pause long enough in their garrulousness to say firmly, "You don't like me, do you?" So Bogart was not a man ever to flatter or—what was harder in his last year—to sympathize with.

Before I saw him for the last time, in the late spring of 1956, I had had from a surgeon friend the dimmest prognosis of his condition, which was that of a man still receiving massive doses of X-ray treatment after an operation for cancer of the esophagus. "Cancer of the esophagus," my friend told me, "has a mortality rate of 100 percent." I was sorry to have heard this, for it was going to be hard to keep up the usual banter. But it turned out that there was no strain of any kind because, I believe, he knew the worst and had months before resolved to rouse himself for two hours a day to relax with a few intimate friends before the end came. Most of us never knew for sure that he had been for many months in abominable pain. Another of his triumphant deceptions was that he managed to convince everybody that he was only intermittently uncomfortable. Throughout the spring, he remained a genial skeleton, and when I went up there the last time, at the beginning of June, his wife was off talking to a journalist friend, and a lawyer was leaving Bogart, who had just finished his will. Whether his wife knew about this I am unsure, but he spoke of it to me, and of his illness, and the sudden uselessness of money, with an entirely unforced humor and an equally unforced seriousness; neither with complaint nor with a brave absence of complaint.

Two of his oldest friends came in, Nunnally Johnson and David Niven, and we talked about the coming California primary election, which pitted Senator Estes Kefauver against Adlai Stevenson in the knockout bout for the 1956 Democratic presidential nomination. The popular reputation of the Senator—especially among Stevenson supporters—was that of an earnest, wily, straitlaced, and rather sanctimonious Southern preacher. It seemed a good time to enlighten the assembled company to Kefauver's quite different reputation in the exclusive club of the United States Senate. "True or not," I said, "he has a terrific reputation as a lecher." Bogart nodded as if to say it was no more than you'd expect. Nunnally Johnson was a little more alert and suspected he'd misheard: "Did you say lecturer?" No, I said, "lecher." My God, Bogart cried, "Lecher! I wish to God we could spread the same word about Adlai."

It was, if not a happy occasion, at least a serene and cheerful one. And I was aware of no strain on the part of the company. It is difficult for actors to avoid the dramatizing of their emotional life, whether grossly by "living the part" or subtly by sentimental deprecation. Bogart, it was a vast relief to discover, was merely

232

himself, a brave man who had come to terms, as we all
may pray to do, with the certain approach of death.

In short, a much more intelligent man than most of
his trade, or several others, a touchy man who found
the world more corrupt than he had hoped; a man with
a tough shell hiding a fine core. He had transmuted his
own character into a film persona and imposed it on a
world impatient of men more obviously good. By
showily neglecting the outward forms of grace, he kept
inferior men at a distance. For he lived in a town
crowded with malign flatterers, hypocrites and
poseurs, fake ascetics, studio panders, and the pimps of
the press. From all of them he was determined to keep
his secret: the rather shameful secret in the realistic
world we inhabit, of being an incurable puritan, gentle
at bottom and afraid to say so.

Pictures

Page 8: Charlie Chaplin, photographed by Alistair Cooke aboard Chaplin's yacht the *Panacea* in July, 1933.

Page 50: Edward VIII, then Prince Edward, in his early twenties.

Page 94: H.L. Mencken, photographed by Alfred A. Knopf in the spring of 1939.

Page 134: This photograph of Adlai Stevenson was taken in London on July 14, 1965, only moments before he suffered a fatal heart attack (Wide World Photos).

Page 174: Bertrand Russell on his eighty-fifth birthday, in 1957 (Keystone).

Page 206: Humphrey Bogart in 1950 (Columbia Pictures).

Bestsellers from Berkley
The books you've been hearing about—and want to read

___**THE BIDDERS**   04606-4—$2.75
John Baxter

___**TROIKA**   04662-1—$2.75
David Gurr

___**ZEBRA**   04635-4—$2.95
Clark Howard

___**THE FIRST DEADLY SIN**   04692-3—$2.95
Lawrence Sanders

___**THE THIRD WORLD WAR: AUGUST 1985**   05019-X—$3.50
General Sir John Hackett, et al.

___**THE PIERCING**   04563-3—$2.50
John Coyne

___**THE WINNER'S CIRCLE**   04500-5—$2.50
Charles Paul Conn

___**MOMMIE DEAREST**   04444-0—$2.75
Christina Crawford

___**NURSE**   04685-0—$2.75
Peggy Anderson

___**THE SIXTH COMMANDMENT**   04271-5—$2.75
Lawrence Sanders

___**THE FOUR HUNDRED**   04665-6—$2.75
Stephen Sheppard

___**THE HEALERS**   04451-3—$2.75
Gerald Green

Available at your local bookstore or return this form to:

**Berkley Book Mailing Service
P.O. Box 690
Rockville Centre. NY 11570**

Please send me the above titles. I am enclosing $_____
(Please add 75¢ per copy to cover postage and handling). Send check or money order—no cash or C.O.D.'s. Allow six weeks for delivery.

NAME_____

ADDRESS_____

CITY_____ STATE/ZIP_____ **Z**